Literature
Celebrations:

Catalysts to High-Level Book Responses
• Second Edition •

BERTIE KINGORE
AUTHOR

Jeffery Kingore
GRAPHIC DESIGN

PROFESSIONAL ASSOCIATES PUBLISHING

Other Publications by
Bertie Kingore, Ph.D.

Alphabetters: Thinking Adventures with the Alphabet (TASK CARDS)
Assessment: Time Saving Procedures for Busy Teachers, 2nd ed.
Differentiation: Simplified, Realistic, and Effective
Centers in Minutes! (BOOK AND CD-ROM)
Engaging Creative Thinking: Activities to Integrate Creative Problem Solving
Integrating Thinking: Practical Strategies and Activities to Encourage High-Level Responses
Just What I Need! Learning Experiences to Use on Multiple Days in Multiple Ways
Kingore Observation Inventory (KOI), 2nd ed.
Portfolios: Enriching and Assessing All Students; Identifying the Gifted, Grades K-6
Rubrics and More! The Assessment Companion (BOOK AND CD-ROM)
Teaching without Nonsense: Activities to Encourage High-Level Responses
We Care: A Curriculum for Preschool-Kindergarten, 2nd ed.

FOR INFORMATION OR ORDERS CONTACT:

PROFESSIONAL ASSOCIATES PUBLISHING
PO Box 28056
Austin, Texas 78755-8056
Toll free phone/fax: 866-335-1460

VISIT US ONLINE!
www.kingore.com

Literature Celebrations:
Catalysts to High-Level Book Responses, 2nd ed.

Copyright © 2003 Bertie Kingore

Published by **PROFESSIONAL ASSOCIATES PUBLISHING**

Printed in the United States of America
ISBN: 0-9716233-1-7

TABLE OF CONTENTS

INTRODUCTION _____

Literature Celebrations: Catalysts to High-Level Book Responses is the result of a labor of pure enjoyment. It is such a privilege to bring great children and great books together by sharing activities that engage children's thoughts, feelings, and interests. <u>Literature Celebrations</u> encourages students to respond actively to literature instead of working on simple skills. These responses help children construct meaning and develop an in-depth understanding of the content. Also, these activities assure teachers that students read and think about a book rather than only look at the cover and read the summary.

PURPOSES OF THE STRATEGIES AND ACTIVITIES

- To attract, intrigue, absorb, and completely involve children in wanting to read and learn from books

- To enable teachers to apply practical techniques and activities to stimulate students' thinking with less preparation time

- To provide a variety of simple strategies and activities that connect to a myriad of books and grade levels

- To serve as springboards for discussing and writing more extensively about literature

- To celebrate diversity in thinking by encouraging multiple correct responses at different levels of understanding

- To relate literature to students' lives and experiences

- To replace worksheet activities that require little thinking with active participation tasks that challenge students to generate responses

- To assess the depth and complexity of students' understanding

RESPONSES TO LITERATURE

> *The purpose of school should be to set the idea that there is a book side to everything.*
>
> Robert Frost

Research documents that students benefit from the activities and discussions that accompany reading. Activities that follow reading experiences are most effective when they engage a child's mind, interests, and feelings. Discussing the story and the illustrations helps a child develop a thoughtful

Kingore, B. (2003). <u>Literature Celebrations</u>, 2nd ed. Austin: Professional Associates Publishing.

NOTES   attitude towards reading and facilitates critical, reflective thinking which is the hallmark of advanced literacy.

Responses to literature:

- Help students construct meaning and deepen understanding of what was read.
- Encourage students to revisit the literature.
- Promote literacy development and skill transfer.
- Enable students to demonstrate their levels of understanding.
- Enable teachers to assess and evaluate.

Responses to literature should be:

- Content-rich rather than just fun or cute.
- An authentic match to a given piece of literature.
- Open-ended to encourage individual levels of readiness and diverse interpretations.
- Teacher-guided when needed.
- Self-selected when possible.

Adapted from the research of: Altwerger, et al. (1987), CIERA (2001), Cooper (1993), Krashen (1993), National Reading Panel (2000), Smith (1990), Strickland (1998), Trelease (1995), and Veatch (1996).

> *The more you read, the better you get at it; the better you get at it, the more you like it; and the more you like it, the more you do it. The more you read, the more you know; and the more you know, the smarter you grow.*
>
> Jim Trelease

SELECTING LITERATURE

Think about these ideas as you select quality books to use in your teaching.

- It is an asset if a book relates to the instructional topics and objectives for your grade level. However, many books deserve to be shared just because they are so enjoyable.

- Literature is generally not intended to be applicable to only one grade level. Most great books can and should be used by multiple grade levels to allow students to revisit favorites and benefit from the increased insights they develop with age.

- Preread any book you are considering, and be sensitive to possible objections in some stories. Something as innocent as a child's name used for a negative character can affect a child in your class in an unintentional way.

- Keep reading. Librarians and media specialists are valuable assets in your continuous search for great literature. The web sites at the end of this book are another useful resource. You will discover new titles to add to your book lists and inspire children with your enthusiasm for reading.

- The following checklist helps evaluate the appropriateness and difficulty level of a book for specific students. Use the checklist individually or collectively as you consider new selections with your colleagues.

Evaluation of Appropriateness

1. Judge the overall quality of the book (characters, plot, language, illustrations).
   ❏ high   ❏ moderate   ❏ poor

2. Estimate the number of difficult or unknown words.
   ❏ many   ❏ few   ❏ none

3. Consider the amount of text depicted by the illustrations.
   ❏ most of the text   ❏ some of the text   ❏ little of the text

4. Estimate the students' familiarity with the topic or the story line.
   ❏ high   ❏ moderate   ❏ low

5. Estimate the familiarity of the concepts.
   ❏ familiar   ❏ less familiar   ❏ unfamiliar

6. Consider the textual aids to comprehension.
   ❏ frequent rhyme   ❏ little rhyme   ❏ no rhyme
   ❏ frequent repetition   ❏ little repetition   ❏ no repetition
   ❏ predictable pattern   ❏ little use of pattern   ❏ no language pattern

7. Consider the application of the book to instructional topics and objectives.
   ❏ high   ❏ moderate   ❏ low

8. Estimate the interest level.
   ❏ high   ❏ moderate   ❏ low

Kingore, B. (2003). Literature Celebrations, 2nd ed. Austin: Professional Associates Publishing.

NOTES

INCREASING THINKING WITH ANY GOOD BOOK

Open-ended tasks and questions for literature are organized in this section according to Bloom's Taxonomy of Thinking Skills. These prompts enable teachers to integrate thinking skills with less preparation time and improve their effectiveness in encouraging complex responses and high levels of thinking from students. For easy use, copy and laminate the pages of literature prompts back-to-back to keep with your planning book. The prompts are then conveniently available when new ideas are needed to uplift thinking about a favorite piece of literature or when you find a new book and need ideas for how to use it best. Two examples using these prompts are shared on the next page.

Benjamin Bloom categorized thinking skills into six classifications ranging from the most basic (knowledge) to the most complex (evaluation). Using Bloom's Taxonomy is like constructing a staircase--each level serves as the foundation upon which the next level of thinking is built. More specifically, just as you could not build the fourth step of a staircase without the first three steps already in place, students cannot analyze something about which they have no knowledge, comprehension, or application. However, you do not have to start at the beginning levels of Bloom's on any learning experience for which children already have the background to respond at a higher level. Bloom's Taxonomy is intended to enable instruction to begin at the children's highest level of readiness.

EVALUATION
SYNTHESIS
ANALYSIS
APPLICATION
COMPREHENSION
KNOWLEDGE

An activity's level is designated at the Bloom's level that most students are likely to achieve. Individual students may operate above or below that level, depending upon the amount of thinking each applies to the task. For example, during an analysis task, a student who uses that analysis to create a unique idea, mentally moves to syntheses. However, if no analysis occurs, the student is only operating at the application level or lower. The levels of synthesis and evaluation are used after a teacher ensures that students have analyzed information.

Upper-elementary and middle-school teachers may want to provide a copy of some or all of the Bloom's literature prompts to the students. Students are then able to self-select questions and task responses for themselves or their groups. These prompts may be particularly useful to the Discussion Director of the literature circle (see the Literature Circles section).

Adapted from: Kingore. (1999). Integrating Thinking.

Kingore, B. (2003). Literature Celebrations, 2nd ed. Austin: Professional Associates Publishing.

The Gardener

KNOWLEDGE

1. Who are the main characters in the story?
2. List two things that happened in the story.

COMPREHENSION

1. How does Lydia feel about living in the city?
2. What can you see, hear, smell, or feel as you read this story?

APPLICATION

1. Pretend you are Lydia Grace, and write Uncle Jim a letter to thank him for taking care of you.
2. Role play the responsibilities that Lydia has in the story.

ANALYSIS

1. How do Uncle Jim's feelings about Lydia living with him change from the beginning to the end of the story?
2. In what way is Lydia like her garden?

SYNTHESIS

1. Create and tape record another story about this character telling what happens after this story.
2. Draw a plant to symbolize each character. Explain why each plant symbolizes that character.
3. Add yourself to the story as Lydia's friend who still lives in the country. Write Lydia a letter about your experiences at home and then write Lydia's response.

EVALUATION

1. What values are being shared in the story? How are those values a part of your life?
2. Discuss three reasons why this book is better than _____ (another book) _____ .

Stewart, S. (1997). The Gardener. New York: Farrar Straus Giroux.

Silent to the Bone

KNOWLEDGE

1. Who are the main characters in this story?
2. What are two major events important to the story?

COMPREHENSION

1. List three words used to describe Branwell.
2. What are two other words that mean the same as epiphany?

APPLICATION

1. Create an illustrated time line to show the book's events in the order they actually occurred instead of the flashback technique used by the author.
2. Illustrate or act out the climax of the story.

ANALYSIS

1. What is the message implied by the story?
2. How are the characters, setting, or problems connected to your life?
3. Why did the author tell the story from the friend's point of view?

SYNTHESIS

1. How did the author use language to evoke images?.
2. Why did the author use the word "bone" in the title? Create a different title that reflects your emotional response to the story.

EVALUATION

1. Which five adjectives best describe the plot of this novel? Defend your choices.
2. Who is the most powerful character in this book? Explain your criteria, and defend your decision.

Konigsburg, E.L. (2000). Silent to the Bone. New York: Aladlin.

Kingore, B. (2003). Literature Celebrations, 2nd ed. Austin: Professional Associates Publishing.

RESPONSE PROMPTS FOR YOUNGER STUDENTS: _____
INCREASING THINKING WITH ANY GOOD BOOK

KNOWLEDGE
1. What is the name (title) of this story?
2. Who is the main character?
3. What is one thing that happens in this story?
4. Tell me two things used/found in the story.
5. _____

COMPREHENSION
1. Write a list of words to describe the main character.
2. What is the meaning of this word as it is used in the story: _____?
3. What happens first?
4. Use these pictures to show something that happens at the beginning, the middle, and the end of the story.
5. Retell the story in your own words.
6. Write another word that means the same as: _____.
7. Arrange these four scenes on the felt board in the sequence of the story.
8. You have one card with "Yes" on it and one card with "No". When I describe something, hold up "Yes" if it is in this story, and hold up "No" if it is not in this story.
9. _____

APPLICATION
1. Use blocks to construct the setting of this story.
2. Draw a map to show _____.
3. Write a letter to a friend about the events in the story.
4. Show how the main character _____.
5. Act out one scene or event.
6. List three items from the story, and tell how they were used to develop the plot.
7. Plan appropriate music to play in the background of one scene.
8. Decorate a book jacket that illustrates an important event in the book.
9. Use play dough or clay to sculpt something important in the story.
10. Create a poster about the author.
11. _____
12. _____

ANALYSIS
1. How are these two characters or events similar, and how are they different?
2. Think about real and fantasy. Use your "Yes" and "No" cards as I describe an event in the story. Hold up "Yes" if it could really happen, and "No" if it could not.
3. What is something you do or feel that is like the main character?
4. How would you solve the problem in the story differently?

Kingore, B. (2003). <u>Literature Celebrations</u>, 2nd ed. Austin: Professional Associates Publishing.

5. Use a Venn Diagram to compare this story to another story.
6. Draw a story map that shows the problem, solution, and main events in the order in which they happen.
7. When or how could the main character use a rope in this story? ...a bucket? ...a ruler?
8. As an animal, the main character would be a(n) _____ because _____.
9. Act out one event from the story for others to figure out and explain what happens next.
10. What other books have similar messages or themes? Explain.
11. What I like best about this book is _____.
12. _____
13. _____

SYNTHESIS

1. Predict what might happen if _____.
2. Add yourself to the original story, and write what you would do.
3. Use cut paper and glue to show the most important event or turning point in the story.
4. Create and tape record another story about this character, telling what happens after this story.
5. Make a collage using symbols for different events in the story.
6. Write a poem about the two main characters that explains how they are different.
7. Draw a symbol for each character, and explain how that character is like that symbol.
8. Make a flap book (see page 33) in which you draw an important cause from the story on the outside of the flap and the effect on the inside.
9. Create an award for this book, and explain why this book deserves this award.
10. Which sound effects, props, and actions best represent this story? Use them to act out this story for others.
11. _____
12. _____

EVALUATION

1. What would your family think of this story? Why?
2. Make up a rating system, and rate this book. Explain your idea.
3. Which character is most important to the story? Why?
4. What would you say to convince the librarian to put this book in the library?
5. Make this book into a movie.
   a. What will be the title and setting?
   b. Who will star in the movie?
   c. Which three scenes are most important to show in the movie? Why?
6. Write a review of this book for a local newspaper, evaluating the book's appropriateness and appeal to readers.
7. Discuss three reasons why this book is not as good as ____(another book)____.
8. Discuss three reasons why this book is better than ____(another book)____.
9. _____
10. _____

Kingore, B. (2003). Literature Celebrations, 2nd ed. Austin: Professional Associates Publishing.

RESPONSE PROMPTS FOR OLDER STUDENTS: _____
INCREASING THINKING WITH ANY GOOD BOOK

KNOWLEDGE
1. Who is the author?
2. Who are the main characters?
3. Name two important events in the story.
4. List two other books by this author or about this subject.
5. _____

COMPREHENSION
1. List three words from the story used to describe the main character.
2. Describe what led to a character's actions.
3. State something that happened in the beginning, the middle, and the end of the story.
4. What are two other words that mean the same as _____ as it is used in the story?
5. Write a three-sentence summary of the story.
6. What is the correct sequence of these five events?
7. _____

APPLICATION
1. Create an illustrated time line to show _____.
2. Write a letter to a friend about how the book affected you.
3. Illustrate the turning point or climax of the story.
4. Demonstrate how the main character uses _____ in the story.
5. Act out one scene or event involving two main characters.
6. Draw a comic strip or story board relating the main events of the story.
7. Select music to play in the background of one scene, and explain why you chose it.
8. Create a poster that details the author's life and background.
9. _____

ANALYSIS
1. Name two characters, events, or books by this author. How are they similar/different?
2. Identify which parts of the story are real or fantasy, fact or opinion. What in the print supports that?
3. Using a Venn diagram, compare the main character with yourself.
4. How would the story change if told through another character's point of view?
5. How would you solve the problem in the story differently?
6. The main character or topic is like a(n) _____ because _____.
7. Pose two unanswered questions about the story.
8. What is the main idea? What is the message implied by the story?
9. Select three songs that symbolize either the main character or the main idea.
10. On a concept map, illustrate one character's reactions and relationships.
11. What other books have similar messages/themes? Explain.

Kingore, B. (2003). Literature Celebrations, 2nd ed. Austin: Professional Associates Publishing.

12. Compare this author's style to the style of your favorite author.
13. Complete a story map relating the problem, sequence of events, and solution.
14. _____

SYNTHESIS

1. What might happen if the main character had been a different gender?
2. Add yourself to the original story or historical time, and write about your role.
3. How did the author use language to evoke images? Create a collage of those words and images.
4. Create a new setting and time for the story. Discuss how it still suits the characters' needs but what changes would have to occur.
5. Create a museum exhibit that incorporates the most significant events in the book. Write brief descriptions of the artifacts and their significance.
6. Write a sequel to the book that reveals how the characters mature.
7. Using symbols for the main idea and events of the story, draw a sequence map that reveals the most significant attributes.
8. Make a collage or mobile using symbols for the characters and events in the story that reveal the major ideas.
9. Write a diamante poem comparing the two main characters.
10. Create a board game based on the most significant characters and events in the book. Design the board to reflect the setting.
11. Create an award for this book. Explain the award's significance and why it is deserved.
12. _____

EVALUATION

1. Write a review of this book for your local newspaper, evaluating the book's appropriateness and appeal for adolescent readers.
2. Judge the characters' actions and thoughts according to your life standards.
3. Did the main character make the right decision? Justify your answer.
4. Would the outcome be plausible in a different setting? Defend your view.
5. After reading the story, assess the values that were modeled, and determine what relationship those values have to people your age.
6. Is the theme relevant for today's culture? Defend your position.
7. Which character is most important to the main idea of the story? Explain the criteria you used, and defend your decision.
8. You are an agent for the author. Convince a publisher to buy this book.
9. Debate whether or not this book will be valued as a classic by future generations.
10. This book is going to be made into a movie.
    a. Create a new title and poster that promotes the message or theme.
    b. Cast the movie, and defend how each of your casting choices matches each character.
    c. Because of budget limitations, one character's role has to be eliminated. Defend which character can be deleted without significantly altering the story.
11. Which five adjectives best describe the plot of this novel? Defend your choices.
12. _____

Kingore, B. (2003). *Literature Celebrations*, 2nd ed. Austin: Professional Associates Publishing.

NOTES

TASK CARDS: BOOK RESPONSES FOR INDEPENDENT WORK

These task cards are designed to engage students' critical and productive thinking when they finish reading a book. The tasks are intended to be completed without direct teacher instruction so some students can work on these learning experiences while instruction is given to others.

This set of cards ranges from simple to more complex. They are not numbered, so they can be arranged according to students' needs. One blank card is included to enable teachers and students to customize learning experiences by creating task cards for additional activities.

Copy the task card pages onto colored paper or cardstock. Then, cut them apart to produce a set of cards. Laminate, hole punch, and connect the cards on a metal ring for management ease. As a set, the cards can be placed in a learning center or used by students at their desks. Choice is a powerful motivator, and many students work more effectively when they can decide among the tasks.

The cards can also be used individually. Post two or more cards on the board or in a pocket chart as product choices for students when they complete a book. Select cards that range in difficulty to customize responses at students' various readiness levels and interests.

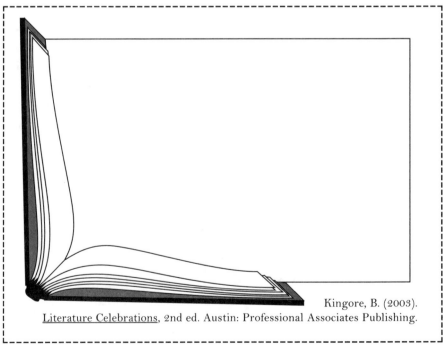

Kingore, B. (2003). Literature Celebrations, 2nd ed. Austin: Professional Associates Publishing.

Literature Connections

Kingore, B. (2003). Literature Celebrations, 2nd ed. Austin: Professional Associates Publishing.

Puppets

Make puppets that represent the main characters. Write a short script, and share the story as a play.

Kingore, B. (2003). Literature Celebrations, 2nd ed. Austin: Professional Associates Publishing.

Cereal Box

Cover a cereal box with paper. Design a new cereal box with illustrations and information about the story. Include the "ingredients" (characters, setting, problem, events, and solution) and "nutritional value" (opinions and ratings).

Kingore, B. (2003). Literature Celebrations, 2nd ed. Austin: Professional Associates Publishing.

Recording Studio

Tape record yourself reading the story. Include a sound effect to signal when to turn the page. Label the tape with the book title and author before you put the tape in the listening center.

Kingore, B. (2003). Literature Celebrations, 2nd ed. Austin: Professional Associates Publishing.

Diorama or Mobile

Construct one or more three-dimensional scenes depicting the story's characters, setting, problem, events, and solution.

Story Board

Develop a story board that illustrates the sequence of the most important events in the story.

Rebus Story

Draw pictures or use cutouts from magazines to write three to five rebus sentences that retell the story.

Flap-Strip Book

Make a flap-strip book. Write the title of the book on the first strip. Then, write beginning, middle, and end on the remaining flaps. On the inside, describe or illustrate what is on each flap.

Games

Develop a Jeopardy!™ or trivia game based upon one or more books. Be the game show host, determine point values for each question, and challenge others to be contestants.

Kingore, B. (2003). Literature Celebrations, 2nd ed. Austin: Professional Associates Publishing.

Creative Dramatics

Determine simple, available props. Act out a scene or the story for another class. As an alternative, pantomime a scene and ask your classmates to explain which event it represents in the book.

Kingore, B. (2003). Literature Celebrations, 2nd ed. Austin: Professional Associates Publishing.

Time Line

Work as an investigator. Complete and illustrate a detailed time line of the events that affect the main character or a minor character who influences the plot.

Kingore, B. (2003). Literature Celebrations, 2nd ed. Austin: Professional Associates Publishing.

Rap

Write a rap or rhyming song that relates the main events of the story and ends with the theme or moral. Perform it for your class.

Kingore, B. (2003). Literature Celebrations, 2nd ed. Austin: Professional Associates Publishing.

Powerpoint

Pretend you are a book critic who is going to give a speech. Create a powerpoint presentation about the author or the story that explains what you like or dislike and why.

Kingore, B. (2003). *Literature Celebrations,* 2nd ed. Austin: Professional Associates Publishing.

Newspaper

Work with others to create a newspaper about the book. Include a front page, want ads, editorials, advertisements, obituaries, sports, and comics that are appropriate for the content of the book.

Kingore, B. (2003). *Literature Celebrations,* 2nd ed. Austin: Professional Associates Publishing.

Readers Theater

Add a narrator to the list of characters, and then rewrite the story to perform as a readers theater. Include expressive dialogue, gestures, and sound effects. Perform for a class or parents.

Kingore, B. (2003). *Literature Celebrations,* 2nd ed. Austin: Professional Associates Publishing.

E-mail

Write a coded E-mail that is exactly 20 words and offers a warning or your advice to one of the main characters. Explain the coded words you chose and their significance to the story.

Kingore, B. (2003). *Literature Celebrations,* 2nd ed. Austin: Professional Associates Publishing.

Story Telling

Dress as a wandering minstrel of the Middle Ages and perform your version of the story. Plan key scenes and big gestures to please and entertain the court.

Kingore, B. (2003). *Literature Celebrations*, 2nd ed. Austin: Professional Associates Publishing.

Video Premier

You have been hired by Hollywood. Form a small group and work together to create a movie of the book. Have a movie premiere and serve popcorn.

Kingore, B. (2003). *Literature Celebrations*, 2nd ed. Austin: Professional Associates Publishing.

Sequel

Continue the author's vision. Write a sequel to the story about the main character, or write a story about the setting after the main character leaves.

Kingore, B. (2003). *Literature Celebrations*, 2nd ed. Austin: Professional Associates Publishing.

Trial

Work with others to form a judge, jury, and lawyers who conduct a mock trial of a character in the story. Create pieces of evidence to present, and have other characters be witnesses.

Kingore, B. (2003). *Literature Celebrations*, 2nd ed. Austin: Professional Associates Publishing.

Illustrated Venn

Draw the outlines of two main characters or significant events from different books. Overlap the outlines to make three areas for writing. List and illustrate how they are similar and different.

Kingore, B. (2003). *Literature Celebrations*, 2nd ed. Austin: Professional Associates Publishing.

Advertisement

Design an illustrated magazine ad for the story. Include a description of events, critics' reviews, and any awards it has won.

Kingore, B. (2003). *Literature Celebrations*, 2nd ed. Austin: Professional Associates Publishing.

Letters

Pretend you are two of the main characters from the story. Write letters back and forth describing what happens in the story. In the letters, explain the main idea from each character's perspective.

Kingore, B. (2003). *Literature Celebrations*, 2nd ed. Austin: Professional Associates Publishing.

This Is Your Life

Work with others to video, tape record, or perform a "This Is Your Life" program about the main character. Act as other characters describing their parts of the story.

Kingore, B. (2003). *Literature Celebrations*, 2nd ed. Austin: Professional Associates Publishing.

ALMOST-FREE, READ-ALONG TAPES

Read-along tapes are "almost free" when a teacher records each story read aloud in class, accumulating a collection of books. This simple process produces tapes for a listening and recording center without requiring extra preparation time.

Benefits of Almost-Free, Read-Along Tapes
- It is of great value when students are absent and miss a book or chapter of something read aloud to the others.
- It enables children to repeatedly read-along and listen to a favorite book.
- It is useful for children who want something interesting to do after they finish other learning tasks.
- It produces an ever-changing supply of tapes for a listening or reading center.
- It encourages automaticity of high-frequency words as children listen repeatedly to the same text.

Put file-folder labels on each tape identifying both the book title and author. About two dozen tapes are ample to use throughout the year. When the children lose interest in listening to a story recorded earlier, record a different book on the tape. The less expensive tapes save money and are of sufficient quality for this purpose.

Noises or unintended sounds can occur at times during a recording. We learned not to worry about these sounds, as they did not spoil the tape for the children. Our class referred to them as "personal tapes" because we knew no one would have one just like ours!

As added fun, helpers' jobs can be incorporated into this production of class tapes. Each week, one person can be designated as the Musical Director who plans musical interludes to play on the tape before and after the book reading begins. Another

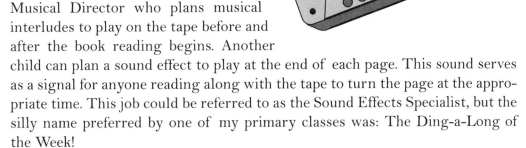

child can plan a sound effect to play at the end of each page. This sound serves as a signal for anyone reading along with the tape to turn the page at the appropriate time. This job could be referred to as the Sound Effects Specialist, but the silly name preferred by one of my primary classes was: The Ding-a-Long of the Week!

Kingore, B. (2003). <u>Literature Celebrations</u>, 2nd ed. Austin: Professional Associates Publishing.
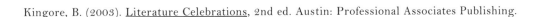

LITERATURE AT HOME

Parents are true partners with schools in facilitating children's literacy development. Parents often ask teachers what to do at home to support their children's reading growth. Some suggestions and parent letters follow.

Family Tapes. Ask family members to record one of their child's favorite books and donate the tape to the class. Even family members who do not live in the area can make a tape to share at school. Children feel proud to have family tapes. It is also an appropriate way to bring a variety of reading voices, dialects, and even different languages into the classroom.

Story Suitcase. One example of a home reading partnership with school is the story suitcase. The children take turns taking home a small suitcase containing a great book to share with the family. The literacy opportunity is augmented by a Traveling Book Journal in which parents and children are encouraged to write a response about the book for the child to share at school on the next day. (Write and date the first, simple entry as a model.) To help family members maximize this reading experience, sample letters to parents explaining a story suitcase, suggestions for reading aloud together, and ways to enrich the reading time and children's comprehension are included on the pages that follow.

There are inexpensive ways to get one or more small suitcases appropriate for this purpose. Families sometimes outgrow small suitcases and will donate them if they know there is a need. Thrift stores and garage sales often have children-sized suitcases inexpensively priced. Also, toy sections of discount stores usually carry small suitcases that can work quite well. If suitcases are not available, a small backpack is an effective alternative. Add a luggage tag to the story suitcase. The luggage tag can include a date for returning the suitcase to school: "Please return me by..."

Any book enjoyed by children in your class can be used in a story suitcase. Some books are particularly appropriate because of their strong family connections. The following are favorites in many families.

Beil, K. (1992). <u>Grandma According to Me</u>. New York: Dell.
Blume, J. (1974). <u>The Pain and the Great One</u>. Scarsdale, NY: Bradbury Press.
Flournoy, V. (1985). <u>The Patchwork Quilt</u>. New York: Dial
Greenfield, E. (1988). <u>Grandpa's Face</u>. New York: Putnam.
Henkes, K. (1991). <u>Chrysanthemum</u>. New York: Trumpet.
Maynard, B. (1997). <u>Incredible Ned</u>. New York: Putnam.
Numeroff, L. (1998). <u>What Mommies/Daddies Do Best</u>. Simon & Schuster.
Penn, A. (1993). <u>The Kissing Hand</u>. Washington DC: Child Welfare League of America.
Taback, S. (1999). <u>Joseph Had a Little Overcoat</u>. New York: Viking.

Kingore, B. (2003). <u>Literature Celebrations</u>, 2nd ed. Austin: Professional Associates Publishing.

Hap E. Ness, Ph. D.

Reading Together: A Family's Cherished Time

Dear Parent,

Parents often wonder what they can do to help their children succeed in school. You are in a unique position to encourage your child to want to read. Children are more likely to associate reading as important when parents make a special effort to read aloud to them. You can:

- Read and enjoy books with your child.
- Be a role model by letting your child see you reading for your own information and enjoyment.
- Provide time for reading, and allow your child to read alone for a few minutes at bedtime. Occasionally, add to the pleasure by providing a flashlight for your child to use to read in bed!
- Read great alphabet books to a young child to build letter recognition and phonemic awareness.
- Read books that provide rich vocabulary and language models that are distinctly different from most television programming.
- Encourage the use of the library as a family.
- Help your child find books and magazines about the interests and subjects he/she is eager to learn.
- Provide another reading model for your child by supplying books for babysitters to share.

Children enjoy time spent reading books with a parent or sibling. Continue reading aloud to children as they begin learning to read for themselves so children do not view independent reading as something that takes them away from "lap time."

The choices you make regarding how you spend time at home with your child sends a clear message to children about what the family values. Thank you for helping your child learn how much you value reading.

Sincerely,

Kingore, B. (2003). Literature Celebrations, 2nd ed. Austin: Professional Associates Publishing.

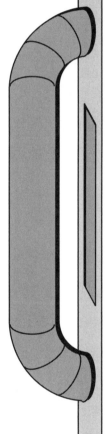

Dear Parent,

Your child has brought home a story suitcase inviting you to read a story together. You make an important contribution to your child's education when you read aloud together.

> *The single most important activity for building the knowledge required for eventual success in reading is reading aloud to children.*
>
> BECOMING A NATION OF READERS

Included in the story suitcase is a good book especially chosen for your child's age and some suggestions for enriching this read-aloud time together. Taking care of the story suitcase can also build your child's sense of responsibility. Please help your child protect the suitcase and its contents so others may enjoy them later.

There is a Traveling Book Journal in the suitcase. You and your child are encouraged to write a note about the book or about reading together. We will help your child read the note to the class tomorrow. Children feel so proud as they tell others about their family times.

Thank you for sharing books with your child. Thank you for sharing your child with us.

Sincerely,

Kingore, B. (2003). <u>Literature Celebrations</u>, 2nd ed. Austin: Professional Associates Publishing.

Reading Aloud to Your Children

Children benefit most from a book when someone talks about the story with them. The following are ways to make a story more meaningful as you read to your child. You might choose one or more of these to try each time you read together.

1. The most important thing is to sit close, smile, and enjoy the time together. Make sure the child can see the pictures easily.

2. Read aloud the name of the author and the illustrator. Talk briefly about what each contributes to the story. Ask if your child remembers any other books by that author or illustrator.

3. Read expressively. Children love it when you "ham it up." Good expression often makes the story even more interesting and increases your child's attention span.

4. As you read, keep your child listening by occasionally asking questions such as: "What do you think is going to happen next?"

5. After the story, talk together and ask your child some of the following:
   - Why do you like or not like the book?
   - Who is your favorite character?
   - What is your favorite part of the story?
   - What is your favorite picture?

6. Later, have your child retell the story to you, using his or her own words.

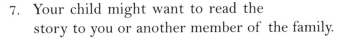

7. Your child might want to read the story to you or another member of the family.

8. Encourage your child to think of different endings to the story.

9. Encourage your child to ask you questions about the story. Your child will think it is fun to make you think of the answers to the questions.

10. Tape record you and your child reading together to replay and enjoy again later.

Kingore, B. (2003). Literature Celebrations, 2nd ed. Austin: Professional Associates Publishing.

MOTIVATING VARIETY

One goal in a language arts program is to encourage students to read extensively from a variety of books. Teachers read great books aloud to students to promote a positive attitude towards reading and stimulate students' interests in a broader variety of topics and genres than they might otherwise know to explore.

To encourage students to read independently from multiple genres, use the Book Filing Cabinet form on the next page. This technique invites a simple response from students that accents thinking about the book while requiring a minimum of handwriting.

Copy the literature genres and topics from the lists below, and then have students cut out and paste three that you or your students want to accent onto the Book File form. After reading each book, students write the book's title, author, and three things about the book that they would like to share with someone else.

Adventure	Drama	Mystery
Animals	Fables	Non-fiction
Autobiography	Fantasy	Poetry
Biography	Historical Fiction	Science Fiction
Contemporary Realism	Humor	Traditional Tale

Adventure	Drama	Mystery
Animals	Fables	Non-fiction
Autobiography	Fantasy	Poetry
Biography	Historical Fiction	Science Fiction
Contemporary Realism	Humor	Traditional Tale

Kingore, B. (2003). Literature Celebrations, 2nd ed. Austin: Professional Associates Publishing.

BOOK FILING CABINET

Read different genres of books. Then, write three things in your book file about each book. Share your ideas with someone else to encourage them to read the book.

TITLE	AUTHOR

Paste the book's genre here.

TITLE	AUTHOR

Paste the book's genre here.

TITLE	AUTHOR

Paste the book's genre here.

Kingore, B. (2003). Literature Celebrations, 2nd ed. Austin: Professional Associates Publishing.

NOVEL STUDY:
AN OUTLINE OF PROCEDURES AND LEARNING EXPERIENCES

Purposes of the Strategies and Activities of this Novel Study

- ***To increase students' active involvement and mental engagement.***
  Students who are mentally engaged are seldomly bored; active involvement increases their learning and personal connections to the novel. The goal is for most of the students to be engaged most of the time. Hence, the emphasis switches from the whole class reading aloud together most of the time to flexible groups working and reading together. Literature Circle techniques can be an effective approach to this goal of active involvement.

- ***To encourage students' high-level responses to their reading.***
  Students and teachers have grown weary of the simple, one-answer literature questions and assignments used in the past. High-level thinking is the right and need of every student, and advanced students prefer higher-thinking responses. The open-ended nature of the tasks outlined in this study challenge all students to become productive thinkers who analyze, synthesize, and evaluate story content.

- ***To apply this outline to other content areas.***
  Activities with multiple opportunities for integration and application are useful to teachers in content areas that use nonfiction text.

I. **Learning experiences before reading**
 A. Activate the students' prior knowledge by discussing which of their experiences may be similar to the events in the book, materials relevant to the topic, and other familiar books by this author.
 B. Build background for the book.
   1. Share interest-grabbing information about the book.
   2. Read aloud poetry and picture books that correlate with the theme or setting of the novel, e.g., the picture book The Yellow Star by Carmen Agra Deedy (2000, Atlanta: Peachtree) integrates powerfully with Lois Lowry's Number the Stars (1989, New York: Dell).
   3. Provide introductory information about the author. (Avoid extensive elaboration so that students retain the option to do research.)
 C. Explain the purposes for reading and how the novel relates to class objectives.

Kingore, B. (2003). Literature Celebrations, 2nd ed. Austin: Professional Associates Publishing.

D. Generate on-going interest by introducing visual tools for the class to cooperatively complete as the novel study progresses.

1. ***ALPHABET CHART.*** List the alphabet down the left-hand margin of chart paper. Challenge students to complete sentences that specify significant information related to the novel for each letter of the alphabet. Students determine two or three different letters to complete for each chapter.

2. ***CHARACTER PROFILE.*** Provide, or have students prepare, large profiles of the heads of the protagonist and antagonist. As the novel is read, students suggest traits or characteristics to add, graffiti style, to the profiles.

3. ***POWERPOINT.*** For each chapter, different small groups of students prepare one part of a cooperative powerpoint presentation about the novel.

II. Guidelines while reading

A. Incorporate techniques that monitor students' reading and encourage high-level thinking.

1. ***REFLECTIVE QUESTIONS.*** Reflective questions (such as those on page 30) focus students' high-level thinking and reactions to their reading. Students store a copy of the questions in their work folder and are responsible for selecting and responding to one or more questions as different parts of the novel are completed.

2. ***NOVEL LOGS AND POWER VERBS.*** Students make slot books (see page 35) or have spiral notebooks to use when writing reactions and responses for each chapter of the novel. Prevent students from simply listing details, i.e., "The first thing that happened..." by providing a short list of powerful verbs that students are required to use in each sentence of their responses. (Students can use additional verbs as long as one power verb is also used in each sentence.) Some effective power verbs are included on the clipboard to the right as an

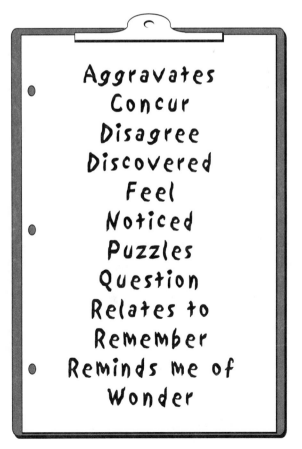

Aggravates
Concur
Disagree
Discovered
Feel
Noticed
Puzzles
Question
Relates to
Remember
Reminds me of
Wonder

Kingore, B. (2003). <u>Literature Celebrations</u>, 2nd ed. Austin: Professional Associates Publishing.

NOTES

example. Encourage students to also incorporate art in their logs to embellish their responses.

3. ***MESSAGE BOARD.*** Using the class' on-line message board, students periodically post observations, reactions, and questions about their reading. Encourage students to post responses to others' messages. (If a website is not available, use a cork board or bulletin board.)

B. Develop students' vocabulary by responding to and building upon the language of the novel.

1. ***GOOD TO KNOW.*** Students need to actively focus on the vocabulary of the book instead of only the teacher providing vocabulary lists of uncommon, multisyllable words for the class to learn. As students read, they search for words that would be useful or important to their vocabulary. When the class meets to discuss the novel, students suggest words they think should be accented. Peers discuss the word and add it to a Good to Know word wall or board when they agree on the value of the word. Preparing and signing a nomination slip such as the one below encourages students to think about vocabulary before presenting it to the class. Challenge students to incorporate these words into their writing and discussions.

2. ***VOCABULARY DISCUSSIONS.*** Prompt students' analysis of the language of the novel with questions that require high-level thinking.

   a. How did the author's language affect the beginning and ending of the novel?

   b. What phrases or sentences within the novel are particularly interesting or surprising?

   c. What are examples of words that are vivid or strong?

   d. How did the author use language to evoke images? What are some of the images?

- -

Nomination Slip: Good to Know

WORD _____ PAGE _____

I/we nominate this word as a good word to know. It is useful or important to us because:

NOMINATED BY: _____ DATE _____

Kingore, B. (2003). Literature Celebrations, 2nd ed. Austin: Professional Associates Publishing.

e.   What are some interesting examples of figurative language?

f.   Where did the author use description effectively?

3.   **IDIOMS.** Analyze the idioms or any special language used by the characters.

4.   **TEXT ANALYSIS.** Invite students to use the Word Wizard form (see page 73).

5.   **FIGURATIVE LANGUAGE.** Encourage high-level thinking by incorporating figurative language responses. Create direct and personal analogies that respond to the text.

a.   __(item from the novel)__ is like __(item)__ because...

b.   __(character)__ is like __(item)__ when...

c.   I am like __(character)__ because...

C.   Motivate class discussions about the novel's ideas and literary elements.

1.   **QUESTIONING.** Teachers and students can pose original questions for discussion or use the response prompts listed (see pages 6-9) and the Reflective Questions (see page 30) to help them with ideas for potential questions.

2.   **PASSAGE INVESTIGATORS.** Individually or in pairs, students take turns preparing passages to share and discuss with the class. (A passage is typically an event or scene that is longer than one page but shorter than a chapter.) The investigators prepare by practicing expressive reading and by writing a brief response that ends with questions to pose to the class. Invite students to use the Text Inspector form (see page 72).

Passage Investigation

PAGES OF THE PASSAGE: _____

CHARACTERS INVOLVED: _____

Three key words for this passage:	Three questions about this passage:

---

3.   **DISCUSSION GRAPHICS.** Skimming the Graphics for Book Responses section of this book, select pages for individuals or small groups to use to focus thinking for class discussions.

4.   **PANTOMIME.** Groups pantomime part of a scene and freeze the action before the scene concludes. The class discusses the conclusion of the scene and their interpretations. As a variation, add a "stop action" element in which a classmate touches an actor's

Kingore, B. (2003). Literature Celebrations, 2nd ed. Austin: Professional Associates Publishing.

NOTES

shoulder to freeze the action and then takes over the character at that point in the scene.

D. Provide shared reading experiences in small groups by inviting students to read aloud selected passages for enjoyment or discussion.

E. Encourage students to initiate conferences in small groups or with the teacher. The following questions are posed as discussion starters.

1. What was your first impression of this novel?
2. Tell me about what you have read so far.
3. If you had a chance to talk to the author or main character, what would you say?
4. What excites or bothers you about this book?
5. What is one thing in this book that is similar to something in your life?
6. What is the main thing you have gotten out of this book so far?
7. Would you recommend this book to anyone else to read? Why?

III. Culminating tasks after reading

A. Culminating tasks should invite students to revisit the literature and respond with high-level thinking. The response prompts (see pages 6-9), task cards (see pages 10-16), and activities in the graphics section of this book provide engaging learning experiences. Consider the following for additional culminating tasks.

1. ***ACROSTICS.*** Write a character's name, the book's title, or a concept word vertically on a page and use each letter to organize connected ideas about the book.

2. ***VENN DIAGRAM.*** Develop a Venn diagram that compares the beginning of the book to the end of the book or the antagonist to the protagonist.

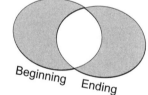

3. ***SIAS.*** In E.L. Konigsburg's <u>Silent to the Bone</u> (2000, New York: Aladdin) the main characters challenge each other to "summarize in a sentence". How would you SIAS this novel?

4. ***NEWSPAPER SCAVENGER HUNT.*** Find something in today's newspaper that relates to this book, e.g., a story with a similar theme, a person expressing feelings similar to the main character, an item that would be useful to one character, or an ad for something needed in the book.

5. ***ABC AUTHOR STUDY.*** Use the alphabet to organize information researched about the author. Include how the author's background and life affected the novel. Try to complete a sentence or paragraph for each letter of the alphabet.

Kingore, B. (2003). <u>Literature Celebrations</u>, 2nd ed. Austin: Professional Associates Publishing.

6. **ABC BOOK RESPONSE.** Retell and respond to the novel by completing a sentence or paragraph for each letter of the alphabet.

7. **NOVEL BOOK BAG.** In a lunch-sized paper bag, place six to ten items that represent the books' content, characters, and theme. Focus on symbols rather than literal items and challenge others to interpret your choices.

8. **FLAP BOOK.** Make a four page flap book (see page 33). On the outside of one of the flaps, write "Summary", and on the inside, complete a summary of the book. On a second flap, write "Key Characters", and on the inside, list the main characters, including a symbol and your insight for each. Next, write "Symbol", and on the inside, draw and explain your best symbol for the theme. Finally, write "Main Ideas", and on the inside, explain one or more major ideas of the novel.

B. Integrating Research. Extend the novel by integrating research that relates to the content or setting. A page of research ideas is on page 31. Use the page when discussing research possibilities with the class, or give a copy to individuals or small groups of students as options to discuss and select as their research focus.

IV. Assessment and evaluation techniques

A. Reflective questions, similar to several on the next page, can be assigned for written responses of a paragraph or page in length. The responses can be graded using the evaluation rubric also on page 30.

B. The task evaluation form is a simple rubric that can be used to grade oral or written products. Its generic nature makes it applicable to many different assignments completed during the course of the novel study. Fill in the type of task at the top and add your preferred grade scale in the shaded area, e.g., letter grades, percentages, or evaluative words such as inappropriate, below expectations, developing, proficient, and above expectations.

C. Develop assessment checklists and other rubrics or an evaluation scale of your choice.

Kingore, B. (2003). Literature Celebrations, 2nd ed. Austin: Professional Associates Publishing.

EVALUATION

TASK: _____

EVALUATION CRITERIA:
- Accuracy of information
- Specific vocabulary
- Depth of content
- Complexity of information

GRADE

- No comprehension is demonstrated

- Attempted a response
- Little evidence of content knowledge is present

- Limited information is provided
- Beginning-level vocabulary and comprehension
- Limited but accurate content is incorporated

- Information is accurate and reflects understanding
- Vocabulary is specific
- Response is supported with appropriate details
- Analysis is evident

- Provided more information than expected
- Vocabulary is advanced and precise
- Response demonstrates a depth of content; meaningful
- Complex level of analysis and interpretation is reflected in the concepts or information

My product earned this grade because _____

Adapted from: Kingore, B. (2002). Rubrics and More!

REFLECTIVE QUESTIONS

1. How does your verbal or written response show that you know the plot and main ideas?

2. How does your verbal or written response demonstrate understanding of the motivations and traits of the characters?

3. What inferences did you form and how do they indicate clear and logical thinking about the text?

4. What predictions did you make and how did they change?

5. What is one change in the sequence that would dramatically alter the story?

6. What do you think about the novel's point of view?

7. Is it more important to retell the sequence of the events or to relate the text to your own experiences? Explain.

8. What connections to other pieces of literature can you make?

9. What three questions would you ask this author to further your understanding?

10. What is the most important thing you learned while reading this novel?

11. Characterize your level of understanding about this novel on a continuum of one to ten, with one indicating "I feel that I don't understand" and ten representing "I thoroughly understand". Explain.

Kingore, B. (2003). Literature Celebrations, 2nd ed. Austin: Professional Associates Publishing.

INTEGRATING RESEARCH

Integrate research beyond the novel by investigating topics that relate to the content and setting of the story. The following topics and questions are posed as research prompts.

1. Author
What were the education and credentials of the author? How did the author's experiences motivate or influence the novel? How is this book like others by this author? What experiences in the author's childhood and early adult life influenced his or her writing? What is interesting or surprising about this author?

2. Significant events
What events were newspaper headlines at the time and place of the novel? How aware were most people of what was occurring in other areas? What unusual weather or natural phenomenon affected this period? What was the relationship of the nation the novel is set in with other countries in the world?

3. Famous people
Who were the political leaders at the time? Who was in the entertainment spotlight? Who was important in the fields of science, mathematics, literature, or art? How did the people who lived in the setting of the novel regard specific famous people?

4. Lifestyles
What were common occupations during that time? What did people wear to work, at home, or at social events? What leisure activities were popular, and did most people engage in them? What kinds of housing did people have? What did food, travel, and housing cost in relation to typical earnings? How did the majority of the people feel about their circumstances?

5. Fine arts
What were the popular movements in the visual arts, theater, literature, and music? How did the majority of people view the arts at the time? How intricate were the fine arts to people's daily lives? How did the fine arts of the time affect society?

6. Issues
What were the most important issues or conflicts? What concerned the majority of the people? What threatened survival? How did the concerns of the people in the setting of the novel compare to the issues of the rest of the world?

7. Trends
What were the trends in social developments, and how did they affect the daily lives of people? Were changes in the culture happening quickly, or was it not a time of significant change?

8. Inventions
What advancements were being made in science? What effects did the latest mechanical inventions have upon people's daily lives? What needs did the people have that motivated the inventors? What new technology precipitated other inventions of the time?

9. Other
What other aspects of life during the setting of the novel were significant and influential?

Kingore, B. (2003). Literature Celebrations, 2nd ed. Austin: Professional Associates Publishing.

NOTES   # BOOKMAKING

Children typically love to make their own books and are more motivated to write when their final product is in a book they made. Book making particularly appeals to visual, spatial, and/or kinesthetic learners. After modeling how to construct them, even kindergartners can make these books without an adult's help, and using legal size paper will provide them with more writing space.

1. ENVELOPE BOOKS

Students stack several envelopes and staple them together along one end. The outside of each envelope is a place for an illustration, and written pages go inside each envelope.

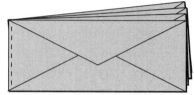

- Staple three envelopes together to create places to write and illustrate the beginning, middle, and end of a story.
- Use one envelope for each character in a story. Students cut out several images from magazine that represent each character to put in the envelopes.
- Use the envelope book to relate a story in sequence or report the sequence of a trip or an experience.
- Create chapter books. Each envelope contains the illustration and text for one chapter of a book a child writes.
- Write imagined correspondence between characters in a novel. For example, Charlotte and Wilbur could write letters from the farm in White's <u>Charlotte's Web</u> (1952. New York: Scholastic.).

2. STAND-UPS

a. Provide large index cards. Students write on several cards and staple the cards together along the top edge.

b. They then cut up other index cards and use construction paper to create cut paper heads and appendages to staple or glue to the top and sides of the first card.

c. Spread the cards apart at the bottom to enable the figure to stand.

- At the beginning of the school year, students construct Stand-ups as a name plate for their desk and write personal facts inside.
- Create a Stand-up that illustrates the main character and analyzes the book's content.
- The cut-paper features enliven research reports about animals, places, and famous people.
- Use the Stand-ups for descriptive, narrative, expository, and how-to process writing.

Kingore, B. (2003). <u>Literature Celebrations</u>, 2nd ed. Austin: Professional Associates Publishing.

3. FLAP STRIP

a. Fold a piece of paper lengthwise (hotdog fold).

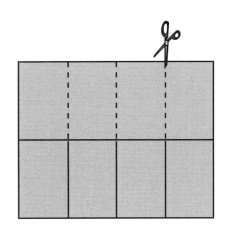

b. Then, fold the paper in half (top to bottom) two more times to create eight equal rectangles like the diagram to the right.

c. Unfold it. On only one side of the hotdog fold, cut the three creases to the center of the paper. This will make four flaps half the width of the page.

d. Fold the four flaps back over. This makes a very simple Flap Strip for young children.

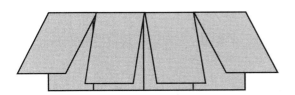

- Write characters, setting, problem, and solution on the flaps. Draw or write inside.
- Write questions about the story on the outside of the flaps and the answers inside.
- On the outside, write or illustrate four important items in the story. Inside, explain why each item is important.
- Draw a continuous mural of the story over all four flaps. Inside each, describe that scene's or image's importance to the story.

4. FOUR-FLAP BOOK

a. Make a Flap Strip.

b. Then, fold the middle two quarters back-to-back and glue them together. (Using a glue stick instead of liquid glue provides a smoother writing surface.

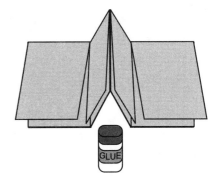

c. Next, close the two outside quarters over so that all flaps are inside the small book.

d. Decorate the outside cover, including the title and author of the story.

- Use the Four-Flap Book instead of the Fold Strip for the suggested activities.
- Have students write sequence words on the outside of each flap, such as first, second, third, and last. Inside, write or draw the story's main events.
- On each flap, students write a cause. Inside, write or illustrate the effect.
- Students write the name and draw a picture of a different character from the story on each flap and then describe the characters or their importance to the story on the inside.

Kingore, B. (2003). Literature Celebrations, 2nd ed. Austin: Professional Associates Publishing.

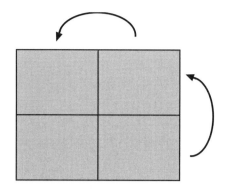

5. TWO-FLAP BOOK

a. Fold a piece of paper lengthwise (hotdog fold) and widthwise (hamburger fold).

b. Unfold the page, and cut along one of the folds to the center of the paper. If the crease along the hotdog fold is cut, the book will be taller. If the crease along the hamburger fold is cut, the book will be wider.

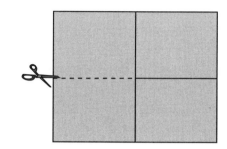

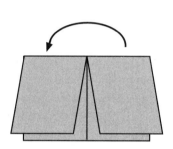

c. Fold the paper in half making two flaps, each a quarter-size of the paper.

d. Close the paper so that the two flaps are on the inside facing each other.

e. Repeat steps a through d with other pieces of paper to make multiple pages for a book.

f. Glue the outside-back of one flap page to the outside-front of another. This will create a book of multiple pages with a flap on each page. Continue connecting flap pages to reach your preferred book length.

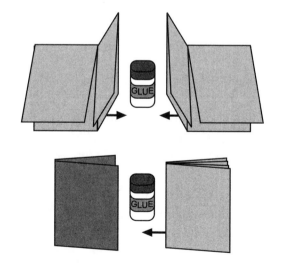

g. Fold a piece of construction paper in the same size and shape of the book. Glue the pages to the inside of the construction paper to create a book cover. Decorate the outside cover, and include the book title and author.

- Use the suggestions for Flap Strips and Four-Flap Books.
- Students retell a story by creating their own book. Encourage them to use a thesaurus to raise the vocabulary level of the original story.
- For more complex thinking, students write summary, key characters, symbols, and main idea on the outside of the flaps and then write and illustrate each inside.
- The Two-Flap book is also an effective form for research reports based on non-fiction sources.

Kingore, B. (2003). Literature Celebrations, 2nd ed. Austin: Professional Associates Publishing.

6. SLOT BOOK

Slot Books are clever creations because they require no glue, tape, or staples to hold the pages together!

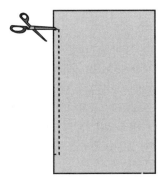

a. Fold two pieces of paper in half. Whether the pages are folded lengthwise (hotdog fold) or widthwise (hamburger fold) is up to the person making the slot book, but both pieces of paper should be folded the same. The hotdog fold produces a taller book. The hamburger fold produces a wider book.

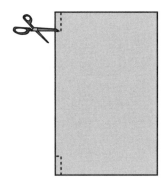

b. On one piece of paper, leave one inch of fold at each end and cut off the rest of the fold in between. This forms the holding slot for the Slot Book. On the other piece of paper, cut a slit one inch long at each end of the fold. This is the slit page that will fit into the holding slot.

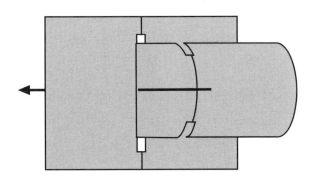

c. Unfold both pieces of paper. Bow the slit page over so that the cut slits match up. Slide it half-way through the holding slot on the other piece of paper. When the folds of both pieces line up, open up the slit page, and fit the slits into the inch of fold at each end of the holding slot.

e. Add as many slit pages to the Slot Book as desired.

NOTE: As slit pages are added, the outside pages that designate the front and back cover of the book will shift.

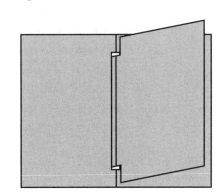

• This book is a favorite for reading logs, book response journals, and original stories.
• It is a very effective product for research reports.
• Use powerful verbs to generate thoughtful responses instead of just reporting details (see page 25). Try response prompts such as: "I noticed..." "I felt..." "I am disappointed..." "I wonder..." "I anticipate that..."

Kingore, B. (2003). <u>Literature Celebrations</u>, 2nd ed. Austin: Professional Associates Publishing.

GRAPHIC RESPONSES

Graphic responses are not meant to encourage a fill-in-the-blank mentality. Rather, they are intended as scaffolds for thinking that allow the responses to be as varied as the students who write them.

The graphic formats in this section are visual tools that guide students' organization of information as they reconstruct a book's meaning. Effectively used, they illustrate the depth of information and the relationship of the ideas or concepts under consideration. Graphic organizers are especially relevant for visual/spatial learners and others who characteristically think in relationships and prefer to organize information in unique ways. The graphics encourage active participation through tasks that challenge students to generate responses rather than just fill in blanks. They are useful for both instruction and assessment as students' levels of responses indicate the depth and complexity of students' understanding.

Several masters for graphic formats are presented in alphabetical order in this section. Initially, introduce the process of using graphic responses as a teacher-directed activity. Specifically, students need assistance and practice to learn how to identify the important information and the relationships among the pieces of information. Deciding what information is important and how to organize the data is a vital process that requires active involvement, increases learning, and helps students construct meaning. Eventually, many students are able to use and complete organizers without direct teacher instruction. A few students may build upon the organizers provided and begin to construct their own graphics.

Teachers sometimes suggest: "I wish I had more time for students to do these fun activities, but I have so many state standards and skills to teach!" Multiple reading skills can be integrated when students thoughtfully complete graphic responses. An alignment of skills to the graphic activities in this book is shared on page 41 as an example. Teams may want to use this format to analyze the skill integration of their instructional choices. Suggestions for incorporating the graphics with language arts instruction and some examples of completed graphics follow.

Ant
The Ant is an appealing graphic organizer with several possible applications.
* Label the three parts of the ant: beginning, middle, and end. Children write story events in each section to retell the story.
* Use the three body segments as a Venn diagram for comparing two stories' similarities and differences.

Kingore, B. (2003). Literature Celebrations, 2nd ed. Austin: Professional Associates Publishing.

- Label the three sections: characters, setting, and plot.
- Label the sections: characters, problem, and solution.

Cause and Effect

Cause and Effect guides students' analysis of the relationships between the major events in a story. After identifying several causes and effects, extend the graphic application.

- Number the causes to indicate their sequence.
- Draw arrows to connect one cause-effect situation that leads to another cause-effect.
- Beside each box, draw illustrations of the character or characters who were a part of that cause or effect.

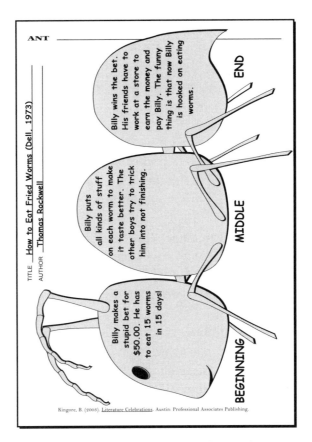

ANT

TITLE __How to Eat Fried Worms (Dell, 1973)__
AUTHOR __Thomas Rockwell__

BEGINNING: Billy makes a stupid bet for $50.00. He has to eat 15 worms in 15 days!

MIDDLE: Billy puts all kinds of stuff on each worm to make it taste better. The other boys try to trick him into not finishing.

END: Billy wins the bet. His friends have to work at a store to earn the money and pay Billy. The funny thing is that now Billy is hooked on eating worms.

Kingore, B. (2003). Literature Celebrations. Austin: Professional Associates Publishing.

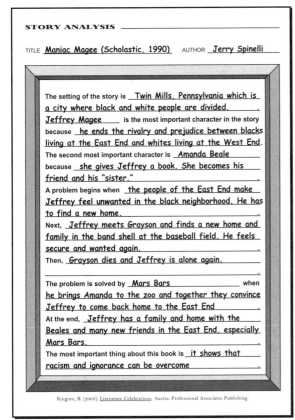

STORY ANALYSIS

TITLE __Maniac Magee (Scholastic, 1990)__   AUTHOR __Jerry Spinelli__

The setting of the story is __Twin Mills, Pennsylvania which is a city where black and white people are divided.__
__Jeffrey Magee__ is the most important character in the story because __he ends the rivalry and prejudice between blacks living at the East End and whites living at the West End.__
The second most important character is __Amanda Beale__ because __she gives Jeffrey a book. She becomes his friend and his "sister."__
A problem begins when __the people of the East End make Jeffrey feel unwanted in the black neighborhood. He has to find a new home.__
Next, __Jeffrey meets Grayson and finds a new home and family in the band shell at the baseball field. He feels secure and wanted again.__
Then, __Grayson dies and Jeffrey is alone again.__

The problem is solved by __Mars Bars__ when __he brings Amanda to the zoo and together they convince Jeffrey to come back home to the East End__
At the end, __Jeffrey has a family and home with the Beales and many new friends in the East End, especially Mars Bars.__
The most important thing about this book is __it shows that racism and ignorance can be overcome__

Kingore, B. (2003). Literature Celebrations. Austin: Professional Associates Publishing.

Character Analysis and Story Analysis

Character and story analysis frames provide a basic content outline to help readers organize information. While the frames appear to be simple, they invite diverse responses and can reveal complex or simplistic understanding. Several applications are possible.

- Have groups work together completing the frames to generate discussions.
- Have students individually complete the frames to assess their comprehension.
- Challenge able students to construct original story frames that focus on specific elements of literature, such as a plot or setting frame.

Kingore, B. (2003). Literature Celebrations, 2nd ed. Austin: Professional Associates Publishing.

NOTES

Facts and Opinions

Pose a problem or question in the center of the graphic. Individually or in small groups, students investigate the text and organize the facts and opinions.

* Document where each fact is supported within the text with page numbers or sticky notes.
* Write or illustrate the person or character who holds each opinion.
* Add "Conclusion" at the bottom of the page. Students discuss and compare their facts and opinions and end by drawing their conclusion.
* Use the graphic at three different points in the story: beginning, middle, and end. Note how opinions change.

Point of View: Character Senses

Characters learn and respond through all of their senses. Prompt students' analysis of point of view by having them complete the graphic from the diverse perspectives of two characters. How would the view of one character differ from what another might see? The following are additional applications.

* As a retelling device, students determine two or three things to list for each sense for each character, for example: "What are three things in the story the protagonist smelled?" Increase complexity and depth by requiring that each example from the story can be used only once.
* Have students work in small groups to list descriptive words that fit story content and match each character's senses.

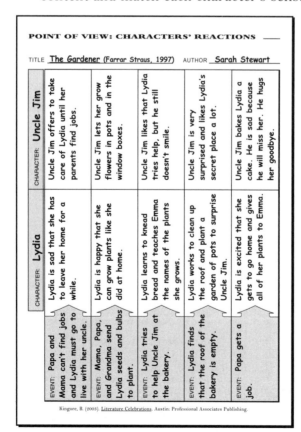

POINT OF VIEW: CHARACTERS' REACTIONS ——

TITLE **The Gardener** (Farrar Straus, 1997)   AUTHOR **Sarah Stewart**

	CHARACTER: **Lydia**	CHARACTER: **Uncle Jim**
EVENT: Papa and Mama can't find jobs and Lydia must go to live with her uncle.	Lydia is sad that she has to leave her home for a while.	Uncle Jim offers to take care of Lydia until her parents find jobs.
EVENT: Mama, Papa, and Grandma send Lydia seeds and bulbs to plant.	Lydia is happy that she can grow plants like she did at home.	Uncle Jim lets her grow flowers in pots and in the window boxes.
EVENT: Lydia tries to help Uncle Jim at the bakery.	Lydia learns to knead bread and teaches Emma the names of the plants she grows.	Uncle Jim likes that Lydia tries help, but he still doesn't smile.
EVENT: Lydia finds that the roof of the bakery is empty.	Lydia works to clean up the roof and plant a garden of pots to surprise Uncle Jim.	Uncle Jim is very surprised and likes Lydia's secret place a lot.
EVENT: Papa gets a job.	Lydia is excited that she gets to go home and gives all of her plants to Emma.	Uncle Jim bakes Lydia a cake. He is sad because he will miss her. He hugs her goodbye.

Kingore, B. (2003). Literature Celebrations. Austin: Professional Associates Publishing.

Point of View: Character Reactions

Students analyze points of view as they list several events in the story and then write comparisons of the reactions of two characters to those events.

* Individually or in small groups, students complete the graphic and then compare and discuss their responses with others.
* Students analyze their personal connections to the story by writing their names in place of one of the characters. They then list key events, write one character's reactions, and complete the graphic with the students' reactions.

Kingore, B. (2003). Literature Celebrations, 2nd ed. Austin: Professional Associates Publishing.

Retelling: Tell It Your Way

Retelling is a strategy that allows students to structure their response according to personal and individual interpretations of the story. Morrow explains that retelling is useful for comprehension, composing a sense of story structure, and measuring language (1989). This simple graphic encourages students to structure their responses using their own words and interpretations of the story. Students are also directed to record interesting words from the story to focus their attention on rich and effective vocabulary that can be applied in future written work and conversations. Consider the following suggestions.

- If young children need something concrete to help them understand beginning, middle, and end, use two bookmarks to divide the book into three sections. Look through each section together and record events on an overhead transparency of the graphic.
- Students can draw and/or write responses to retell the sequence.
- Use the graphic as a prewriting task to organize story content when preparing a written response.

Sequence Map

Sequencing skills are vital to students' comprehension of content and story structure. This graphic accents the sequence of the story and the main idea. In the center, students record key words from the story to focus their attention on rich vocabulary they can use in their written work and in conversations.

- Use the key word area to list words the author used to signal the sequence.
- Discuss how the story might be affected if one element of the sequence changed.
- Use the graphic to illustrate circle stories that begin and end at the same scene.

Story Map

Story Maps require students to analyze and visually represent the relationships among the story elements and the events of the story. This graphic is pictured as a flow chart with one element leading to another.

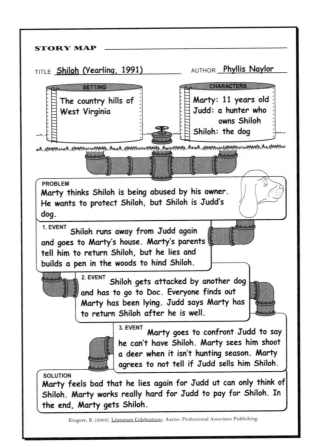

STORY MAP

TITLE _Shiloh (Yearling, 1991)_   AUTHOR _Phyllis Naylor_

SETTING
The country hills of West Virginia

CHARACTERS
Marty: 11 years old
Judd: a hunter who owns Shiloh
Shiloh: the dog

PROBLEM
Marty thinks Shiloh is being abused by his owner. He wants to protect Shiloh, but Shiloh is Judd's dog.

1. EVENT Shiloh runs away from Judd again and goes to Marty's house. Marty's parents tell him to return Shiloh, but he lies and builds a pen in the woods to hind Shiloh.

2. EVENT Shiloh gets attacked by another dog and has to go to Doc. Everyone finds out Marty has been lying. Judd says Marty has to return Shiloh after he is well.

3. EVENT Marty goes to confront Judd to say he can't have Shiloh. Marty sees him shoot a deer when it isn't hunting season. Marty agrees to not tell if Judd sells him Shiloh.

SOLUTION
Marty feels bad that he lies again for Judd ut can only think of Shiloh. Marty works really hard for Judd to pay for Shiloh. In the end, Marty gets Shiloh.

Kingore, B. (2003). Literature Celebrations. Austin: Professional Associates Publishing.

Kingore, B. (2003). <u>Literature Celebrations</u>, 2nd ed. Austin: Professional Associates Publishing.

NOTES

Consider the following application ideas.

- Encourage children to add illustrations to their maps.
- Challenge students to demonstrate their analysis of the characters by using symbols instead of pictures to represent characters.
- Use the map as a prewriting task to organize information from the book.
- Encourage students to incorporate rich vocabulary in their responses.

GENERATING AND RECORDING IDEAS

Clip Board of Thoughts and Piggy Bank of Ideas

Use overhead transparencies of these simple graphics to make a written record of students' ideas before, during, and after reading a book. Later, provide individual copies of the graphics for children to use when brainstorming or responding to a story. Several possibilities for applications follow.

- Write students' predictions about the book as they examine the cover. After reading the story, review their predictions and discuss their ideas.
- Write the group's retelling of a book and model editing it into a strong summary.
- On a second or third reading of a book with rich vocabulary, have young children raise their arms when they hear an interesting word to record on a transparency. These become vocabulary models for use in their writing.

- List questions the group poses as they read the story.
- To expand the story, record the group's prediction of what might happen next if the story continued.
- Record ideas for props and sound effects to adapt the book into a readers theater format for performing.
- Children use the graphics to jot down ideas about a book to share in literature circles.
- Children use the graphics as open-ended reflection forms or story maps.

PIGGY BANK OF IDEAS

TITLE **There's a Nightmare in My Closet** AUTHOR **Mercer Mayer**
(Dial, 1968)

The boy is afraid of the nightmare in his closet. He decides to face it. He isn't afraid when he shoots the nightmare. The nightmare is afraid of him. The boy feels sorry for the nightmare. He lets the nightmare sleep in the bed.

What about the other lonely nightmare? Where will he sleep?

CHARACTER

CHARACTER

A boy is in his bedroom getting ready for bed.

SETTING

Kingore, B. (2003). Literature Celebrations. Austin: Professional Associates Publishing.

Kingore, B. (2003). Literature Celebrations, 2nd ed. Austin: Professional Associates Publishing.

SKILLS ALIGNMENT TO ACTIVITIES

READING	Ant	Cause and Effect	Character Analysis	Clip Board of Thoughts	Facts and Opinions	Piggy Bank of Ideas	Point of View: Characters' Senses	Point of View: Characters' Reactions	Retelling: Tell it Your Way	Sequence Map	Story Analysis	Story Map
Meanings of prefixes and suffixes	•			•		•			•			
Context clues				•	•	•						
Facts and details	•	•	•	•	•	•	•	•	•	•	•	•
Sequential order	•	•		•	•	•		•	•	•	•	•
Complex vocabulary	•		•	•	•	•					•	•
Main idea			•	•		•				•	•	•
Summary	•			•		•			•	•	•	•
Cause and effect		•		•		•		•			•	•
Compare and contrast	•	•	•		•		•	•			•	•
Draw logical conclusions		•	•	•	•	•		•	•	•	•	•
Points of view		•	•				•	•			•	•
Fact and opinion	•	•	•	•	•	•			•		•	

WRITING	Ant	Cause and Effect	Character Analysis	Clip Board of Thoughts	Facts and Opinions	Piggy Bank of Ideas	Point of View: Characters' Senses	Point of View: Characters' Reactions	Retelling: Tell it Your Way	Sequence Map	Story Analysis	Story Map
Inform an audience	•	•	•	•	•	•	•	•	•	•	•	•
Express thoughts	•	•	•	•	•	•	•	•	•	•	•	•
Persuade an audience				•	•	•					•	
Sequencing events or steps	•			•		•			•	•	•	•
Classification	•		•	•		•	•	•				
Develops/supports/elaborates		•		•	•	•		•	•	•	•	•
Complete sentences	•	•	•	•	•	•	•	•	•	•	•	•
Subject, objects, and possessive forms	•	•	•	•	•	•	•	•	•	•	•	•
Subject-verb agreement	•	•	•	•	•	•	•	•	•	•	•	•
Conventions of writing	•	•	•	•	•	•	•	•	•	•	•	•
Figurative language	•			•		•		•				
Rich vocabulary	•	•	•	•	•	•	•	•	•	•	•	•

Kingore, B. (2003). Literature Celebrations, 2nd ed. Austin: Professional Associates Publishing.

ANT

TITLE

AUTHOR

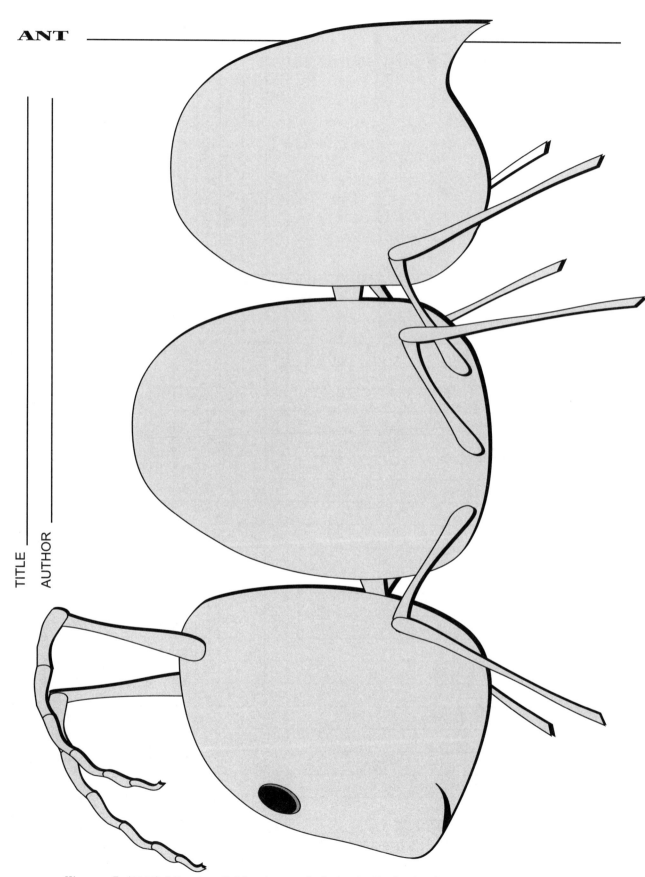

Kingore, B. (2003). <u>Literature Celebrations</u>, 2nd ed. Austin: Professional Associates Publishing.

CAUSE AND EFFECT

TITLE _____   AUTHOR _____

Describe four causes in the story, such as events, characters' actions, or opinions. Then, describe the effects of the causes.

CAUSE:

EFFECT:

CAUSE:

EFFECT:

CAUSE:

EFFECT:

CAUSE:

EFFECT:

CHARACTER ANALYSIS _____

TITLE _____   AUTHOR _____

The most important character in the story is _____

because _____

_____.

The character's primary features are _____

_____.

Three main traits of this character are _____,

_____, and _____.

These traits enable the character to _____

and _____.

The character is in conflict with _____

because _____

_____.

The most important event involving this character is _____

_____

_____.

This event affects the character by _____

_____

_____.

The best thing about this character is _____

_____

_____.

I wish this character _____

_____

because _____.

CLIP BOARD OF THOUGHTS _____

TITLE _____ AUTHOR _____

Kingore, B. (2003). <u>Literature Celebrations</u>, 2nd ed. Austin: Professional Associates Publishing.

FACTS AND OPINIONS

TITLE _____ AUTHOR _____

Problem:

Facts

Opinions

PIGGY BANK OF IDEAS _____

TITLE _____ AUTHOR _____

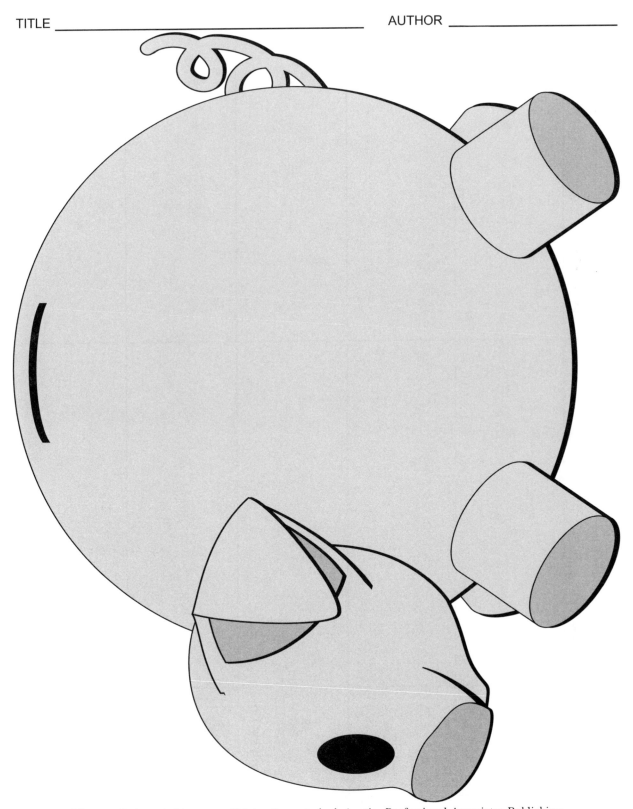

Kingore, B. (2003). <u>Literature Celebrations</u>, 2nd ed. Austin: Professional Associates Publishing.

POINT OF VIEW: CHARACTERS' SENSES

AUTHOR

TITLE

CHARACTER:

CHARACTER:

See

Hear

Touch or Feel

Taste

Smell

Kingore, B. (2003). <u>Literature Celebrations</u>, 2nd ed. Austin: Professional Associates Publishing.

POINT OF VIEW: CHARACTERS' REACTIONS ——

TITLE _____ AUTHOR _____

CHARACTER:				

CHARACTER:

| EVENT: | EVENT: | EVENT: | EVENT: | EVENT: |

Kingore, B. (2003). <u>Literature Celebrations</u>, 2nd ed. Austin: Professional Associates Publishing.

RETELLING: TELL IT YOUR WAY _____

TITLE _____ AUTHOR _____

INTERESTING WORDS USED IN THE STORY _____

BEGINNING

What happens first?

MIDDLE

What happens next?

END

What happens last?

SEQUENCE MAP _____

TITLE _____ AUTHOR _____

SEQUENCE OF EVENTS

1.

2.

Problem:

Key words:

3.

Solution:

5.

4.

MAIN IDEA _____

_____

_____

Kingore, B. (2003). <u>Literature Celebrations</u>, 2nd ed. Austin: Professional Associates Publishing.

STORY ANALYSIS _____

TITLE _____   AUTHOR _____

The setting of the story is _____
_____ .

_____ is the most important character in the story

because _____
_____ .

The second most important character is _____

because _____
_____ .

A problem begins when _____
_____
_____ .

Next, _____
_____
_____ .

Then, _____
_____ .

The problem is solved by _____ when
_____
_____ .

At the end, _____
_____
_____ .

The most important thing about this book is _____
_____ .

Kingore, B. (2003). Literature Celebrations, 2nd ed. Austin: Professional Associates Publishing.

STORY MAP

TITLE _____   AUTHOR _____

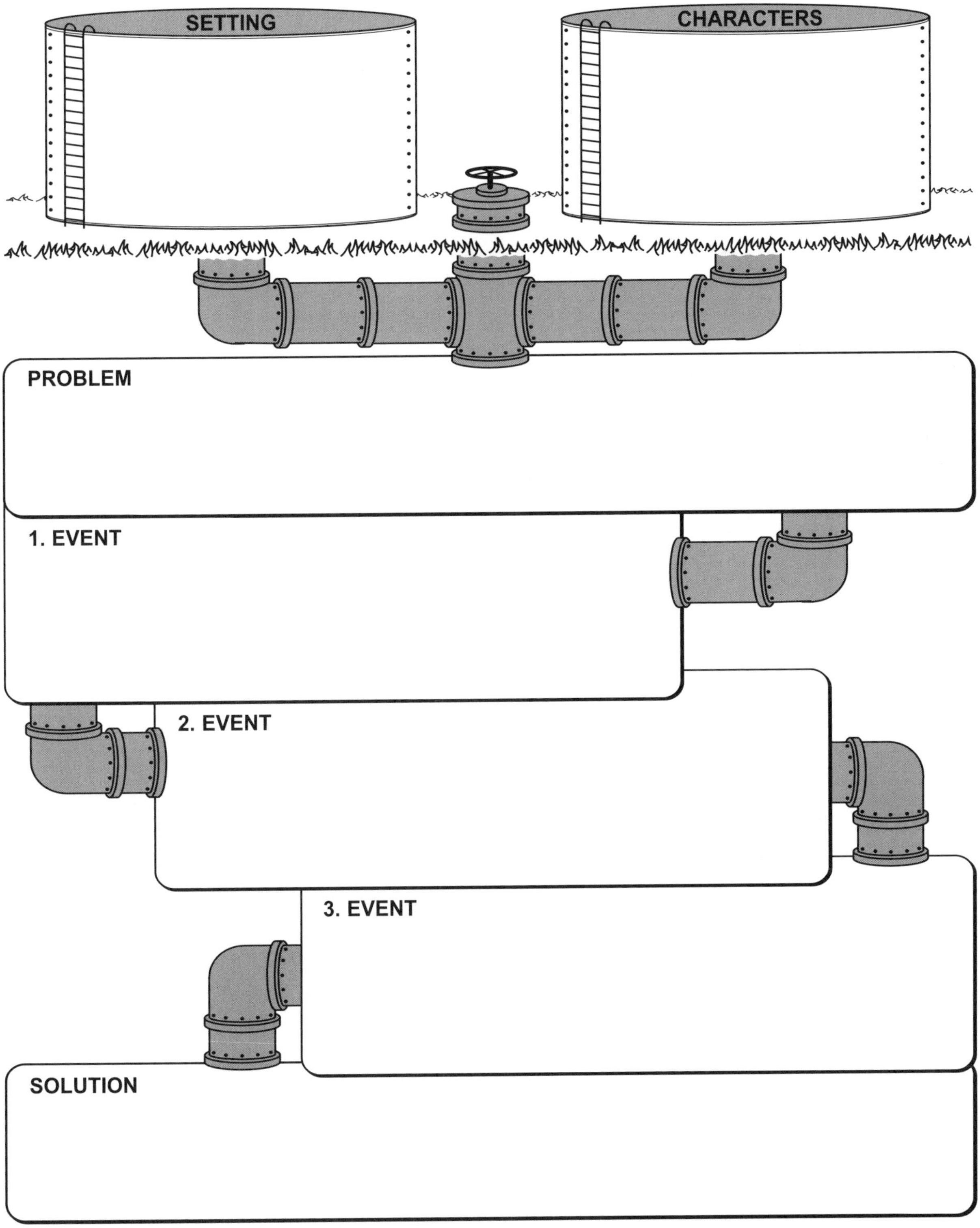

SETTING

CHARACTERS

PROBLEM

1. EVENT

2. EVENT

3. EVENT

SOLUTION

Kingore, B. (2003). Literature Celebrations, 2nd ed. Austin: Professional Associates Publishing.

| # LITERATURE CIRCLES

Literature circles are small, student-centered discussion groups that encourage students to read more and interact with others about what they read. Rather than replace traditional reading programs, literature circles supplement instruction by supporting students' development as fluent readers and high-level thinkers. Researchers support that having students discuss what they read is crucial in developing their ability to construct meaning (Cooper, 1993; Daniels, 1994; National Reading Panel, 2000).

Literature circles are flexible groups of students who have read the same book and typically meet once or twice a week to discuss it. The make-up of the groups change as new books are selected. The dynamics are a treat to behold! Students stretch out on the floor or huddle close together listening and sharing. Their enthusiasm and passion reflect how involved they are with the book. Thus, literature circles provide a balance to teacher-directed groups in which all students are on the same page responding to the teacher's questions. Literature circles help foster a love of reading and can appropriately match the diverse pacing needs and readiness levels of students in a mixed-ability class.

Literature Circles:

- Promote a positive attitude toward reading;
- Provide choice and encourage responsibility;
- Encourage extensive and intensive reading;
- Invite discussions that lead to inquiry and critical thinking;
- Support responses from multiple perspectives;
- Foster interaction and collaboration;
- Nurture reflection and self-evaluation (Owens, 1995).

PROCEDURES FOR USING LITERATURE CIRCLES

Introducing the Circles. Model the process of working in literature circles by initiating one or more of the following.

1. Students are placed in small groups. All groups read the same book as the teacher guides the process.
2. Pair older students with younger students to facilitate as the teacher guides the process.
3. The teacher works with one group at a time to teach the process. When one circle is operating smoothly, model the process with another group until all students are comfortably involved.

Short books work best during this training time as small groups of students simultaneously explore, with the teacher's guidance, many different ways to question and respond to peers about the book. Copy the Literature Circle Behaviors to display prominently as a poster, and then discuss and role play the behaviors together. As the groups finish reading, model a variety of responses such as: "Everyone find and share your favorite part of the story," or "For two minutes, everyone sketch something you think is very important in the story; now explain it to your group." Provide copies of question prompts (see pages 6-9) and invite students to pose questions to others in their group. Give warm comments as you hear an effective question and answer. After successfully introducing the circles, help groups select different books to read.

Literature Circles with Young Students. First and second grade students are enthusiastic about getting together with others to share books they enjoy. As one child explained: "You don't have to write stuff. You just talk!" Primary students typically meet once a week to discuss their book. Some primary groups also want to read the book again together. The following sequence works well to implement literature circles with young readers.

1. Briefly share overviews of the books for the children to consider. Then, leave the books in an accessible place as many young children want to handle the books before they make their decisions. Later that day, children complete their book choice slips. (Duplicate the form on page 58.) Place the children into groups of four to six.

2. Communicate with the families that you will send a book home once a week on a specified day. A parent or sibling at home reads the book to the child and then has the child read it to them.

3. Prepare bookmarks with a simple sentence-stem prompt on each like the ones on the next two pages. Copy the pages back to back so each bookmark has a prompt on the front and the back. Laminate and add a tassel or ribbon at the top to complete each bookmark.

4. Each child selects a bookmark to take home with the book. Students place the bookmark in a place in the book where the story content completes the sentence

Kingore, B. (2003). <u>Literature Celebrations</u>, 2nd ed. Austin: Professional Associates Publishing.

I think...

I agree with...

This shows that...

I like how...

At first I thought that...

I am not sure if...

I love how...

This seems to be...

I wonder if...

I feel...

I compare this to...

I don't like...

I suspect that...

This reminds me of...

I am amazed that...

It would be better if...

I am curious about...

I question if...

I predict...

I wish...

This infers...

I disagree with...

I notice...

I don't see why...

Kingore, B. (2003). Literature Celebrations, 2nd ed. Austin: Professional Associates Publishing.

NOTES

stem. When students meet in their literature circles the next day, they open their books to the marked places and share their responses. Students elaborate with additional details and explain why they selected that passage.

High-quality, visually-appealing literature with rich language is required to sustain young readers' interest and attention in literature circles. Predictable literature that offers rhyme and patterns is also an asset.

Sample Books for Young Readers

Barrett, J. (1998). Things That Are Most in the World. New York: Atheneum.
Campbell, R. (1983). Dear Zoo. New York: Viking Penguin.
McMillan, B. (1996). Jelly Beans for Sal. New York: Scholastic. (Non-fiction)
Numeroff, L. (1998). If You Give a Pig a Pancake. New York: HarperCollins.
Raschka, R. (1993). Yo! Yes! New York: Orchard.
Shannon, G. (1996). Tomorrow's Alphabet. New York: Greenwillow.
Steen, S. & Steen, S. (2001). Car Wash. New York: Putnam's Sons.
Taback, S. (1999). Joseph Had a Little Overcoat. New York: Viking.

Literature Circles with Third through Eighth Grade Students. With older students, the emphasis is on open-ended discussions rather than round-robin reading. When reading a short book, have students read the entire book before coming to their literature circle. With a longer book, students generally agree on the chapters to read before each session together. The following sequence effectively implements literature circles with older readers.

1. Share brief overviews of books for students to consider. Then, leave the books in an accessible area for students to review as they make decisions and complete choice slips. (Duplicate the form to the right.) Use the students' choices to form circles of four to six students.

LITERATURE CIRCLE BOOK CHOICE

NAME _____

DATE _____

First choice:

TITLE _____

AUTHOR _____

Second choice:

TITLE _____

AUTHOR _____

Third choice:

TITLE _____

AUTHOR _____

Kingore, B. (2003). Literature Celebrations, 2nd ed. Austin: Professional Associates Publishing.

2. Each group meets to organize as a group, plans how much to read before each session, and selects which class-modeled activities or role sheets to prepare.

3. Students then work independently to read and prepare their responses.

4. The circle meets once or twice a week to share and respond to the book. At the close of each session, the students decide what needs to be completed before they meet again.

Well-crafted, age-appealing literature has a tremendous influence on older students' depth of conversations and sustained engagement with a book. Dialog, humor, and adventure are also advantageous. Most older children prefer to read chapter books in their literature circles.

A Sample of More Simple Chapter Books

Brown, M. (1998). <u>Arthur</u>. Boston: Little, Brown.

Cleary, B. (1990). <u>Muggie Maggie</u>. New York: New York: Morrow.

Gardiner, J. (1980). <u>Stone Fox</u>. New York: HarperCollins.

MacLachlan, P. (1994). <u>Skylark</u>. (1985). <u>Sarah, Plain and Tall</u>. New York: HarperCollins.

Park, B. (2001). <u>Junie B., First Grader (at last!)</u>. New York: Random House.

Parks, R. with Haskins, J. (1992). <u>Rosa Parks: My Story</u>. New York: Penguin Putnam.

A Sample of Chapter Books with Group Appeal

Konigsburg, E.L. (2000). <u>Silent to the Bone</u>. New York: Aladdin.

Naylor, P. R. (1997). <u>Saving Shiloh.</u> (1996). <u>Shiloh Season</u>. and (1991). <u>Shiloh</u>. New York: Dell.

Sachar, L. (1998). <u>Holes.</u> New York: Farrar, Straus & Giroux. (1990). <u>Sideways Stories from Wayside School</u>. New York: Random House.

Paulsen, G. (1996). <u>Brian's Winter</u>. New York: Scholastic. (1987). <u>Hatchet</u>. New York: Trumpet.

Peck, R. (1998). <u>A Long Way from Chicago</u>. New York: Puffin.

Spinelli, J. (1990). <u>Maniac Magee</u>. New York: HarperCollins.

Finding Copies of Books. Your school's book supply, paperback book clubs, garage sales, and thrift stores are effective sources of small sets of books. Collect books representing a wide range of reading levels to challenge students' diverse reading abilities. If sufficient copies are available, multiple circles can read the same book.

Organization. Determine the number of literature circles you need for groups of four to six. Group students together according to their book choices. Some

NOTES

students select a book to be with friends. Explain to students that being together is appropriate as long as the group is productive. Place the entire class in literature circles at the same time, or rotate groups among different tasks such as working with the teacher, literature circles, and independent work.

Student Responsibilities. Students have the responsibility to be prepared, to be an active participate in their group, and to self-evaluate. Choose one or more of the following ideas to encourage them to read carefully and think about their book.

1. Students use copies of the book marks in this section to mark a place in the book to share with their group.

2. Students select among the role sheets in this section to guide their preparation and sharing. Not every role may be appropriate or needed.

3. Students select or are assigned an activity that has been demonstrated

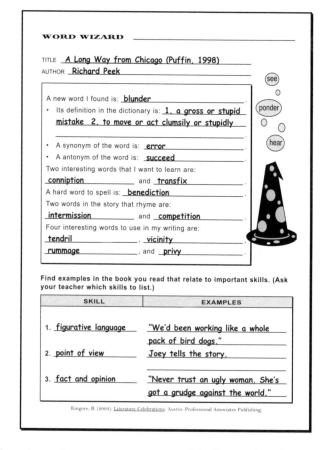

and used previously with the class that can now be used independently as students prepare for their literature circle.

Well-prepared students are better able to actively share ideas and responses to the book. The goal is for each member of the literature circle to participate, pose questions, and discuss insights. To maintain interest, students should prepare different response activities and roles rather than always selecting the same task.

Students are also responsible for self-evaluating using simple formats such as the examples on pages 30, 61, and 63. Add your preferred evaluative scale in the shaded area on each rubric using letter grades, percentages, or evaluative words, e.g. below expectations, novice, developing, effectively done, above expectations. Reflective questions can also be selected by students for their written reflections and evaluations. Examples of reflective questions are shared on pages 27 and 30.

Teachers' Roles. In the past, teachers assumed the major responsibility for guiding literature discussions in the classroom by developing dozens of questions for each novel. Now, teachers find they can save preparation time and shift their role to facilitator. Teachers typically move among the groups, sometimes interacting, often jotting anecdotal notes of observations about the process and skills children demonstrate. Teachers freely join any group experiencing difficulties to help the students refocus their task or direction.

Different versions of students' literature roles are offered to match diverse modality preferences and to provide choice in the difficulty level you deem best for specific students. Use these examples to develop more effective and appropriate roles for your class. Encourage students to experiment with different roles. As they gain experience with literature circles, assignments may no longer be needed to guide interactions.

If grades are required, teachers can assign grades to the completed activities or role sheets. The forms students use for their self-evaluations can also be used by teachers as grade sheets. In addition, teachers can prepare different rubrics to provide a standard for evaluation. Multiple examples of rubrics and efficient procedures for generating rubrics are demonstrated in Assessment: Time-Saving Procedures for Busy Teachers (Kingore, 1999)and Rubrics and More! (Kingore, 2002).

Daniels suggests a binary grading system of either ten points or zero points (1994). Students earn ten points when they come to a circle with their book read and their assignment or role sheet completed. If they are not completely prepared, they earn zero points for that session. The form below allows students to record their points over several days as they complete a novel. These session grades can be combined into a percentage of the overall grade.

Concluding a Literature Circle. When students have completed a book, the group disperses. New groups of students are encouraged to come together with the next book selection. The process is cyclic and the groups are flexible.

Literature Circle Evaluation

NOVEL _____ AUTHOR _____

Each day your literature circle meets, record the date and the score you earned.
Scoring: 10 points   Assigned reading completed. Assignment or role sheet completed.
              0 points   Not completely prepared

DATE	SCORE	DATE	SCORE	DATE	SCORE	DATE	SCORE	DATE	SCORE

Kingore, B. (2003). Literature Celebrations, 2nd ed. Austin: Professional Associates Publishing.

LITERATURE CIRCLE BEHAVIORS

1.   Look at each other.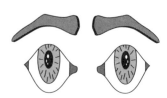

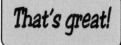 
2.   Quietly say kind and encouraging things.

3.   Help everyone have a chance to share.

4.   Be **friendly,** and **have fun!**

SELF-EVALUATION

TITLE _____

AUTHOR _____

		Poorly	OK	Well
I read the entire book. I marked my favorite parts to share.				
I finished my assignment on time and tried to do my best.				
I thought about my book. I analyzed the content and determined the most important ideas.				
I participated well and shared my ideas with others.				
I gave others a chance to talk. I listened to their ideas and encouraged them.				

One thing I like is _____

_____

Something I would change is _____

_____

This is a good book to read because _____

_____

I earned this grade.

Kingore, B. (2003). Literature Celebrations, 2nd ed. Austin: Professional Associates Publishing.

ANALYZER

Analyze how two characters or events in this story are similar and different.

TITLE _____

AUTHOR _____

I will compare

_____ **to** _____.

▼   **SIMILAR**   ▼

DIFFERENT   **DIFFERENT**

Kingore, B. (2003). <u>Literature Celebrations</u>, 2nd ed. Austin: Professional Associates Publishing.

COMPARER _____

Compare this story to yourself and another book. Use Post-it™ Notes to mark the places in the book that support your responses.

Post-it ™
Notes

TITLE _____

AUTHOR _____

Compared to me!

1. This part of the story is like me because _____

_____

_____

_____

_____

_____

_____ .

2. This character is like me because _____

_____

_____

_____

_____

_____

_____ .

Compared to another book!

3. This part of the story is like

_____ ,
TITLE

because _____

_____

_____

_____

_____

_____

_____ .

4. This character is like _____

_____ ,
CHARACTER

because _____

_____

_____

_____

_____

_____

_____ .

Kingore, B. (2003). Literature Celebrations, 2nd ed. Austin: Professional Associates Publishing.

DISCUSSION DIRECTOR _____

Help everyone in the group have an opportunity to tell their ideas. Encourage quiet people to share.

TITLE _____

AUTHOR _____

Write one good idea that each person shared.

ANALYZER _____

_____

COMPARER _____

_____

ILLUSTRATOR _____

_____

INFERENCE INTERVIEWER _____

_____

INTERVIEWER _____

_____

SEQUENCER _____

_____

STORY MAPPER _____

_____

TEXT INSPECTOR _____

_____

WORD WIZARD _____

_____

At the end of the session, tell each person the idea you recorded.

What did you do to help the group discuss the book? _____

_____

_____

Kingore, B. (2003). <u>Literature Celebrations</u>, 2nd ed. Austin: Professional Associates Publishing.

ILLUSTRATOR

Create an illustration for the book. Draw a picture or cut and paste a collage describing a favorite character, an important event, or the main idea of the story. (Do not use the picture on the book cover.) Add thought bubbles or captions to share feelings or explain the scene.

TITLE _____

AUTHOR _____

INFERENCE INTERVIEWER

Pretend to interview a main character from the story. Write six questions you would ask and infer what you think the character might answer.
Write your inferences from the character's perspective.

TITLE _____

AUTHOR _____

CHARACTER _____

INTERVIEWER: _____
_____?

CHARACTER: _____
_____.

INTERVIEWER: _____
_____?

CHARACTER: _____
_____.

INTERVIEWER: _____
_____?

CHARACTER: _____
_____.

INTERVIEWER: _____
_____?

CHARACTER: _____
_____.

INTERVIEWER: _____
_____?

CHARACTER: _____
_____.

INTERVIEWER: _____
_____?

CHARACTER: _____
_____.

Kingore, B. (2003). Literature Celebrations, 2nd ed. Austin: Professional Associates Publishing.

INTERVIEWER _____

Read your book or a favorite section of your book to two people. Interview them and record their opinions.

TITLE _____

AUTHOR _____

PERSON INTERVIEWED _____ AGE _____

What do you like about the story? _____

_____

_____ .

What would you compare this to? _____

_____

_____ .

Which character is your favorite? _____

Why? _____

_____

_____ .

PERSON INTERVIEWED _____ AGE _____

What do you like about the story? _____

_____

_____ .

What would you compare this to? _____

_____

_____ .

Which character is your favorite? _____

Why? _____

_____

_____ .

Kingore, B. (2003). Literature Celebrations, 2nd ed. Austin: Professional Associates Publishing.

SEQUENCER _____

Draw or list the characters and setting of the story. Then, write the most important events from the beginning, middle, and end of the story.

TITLE _____

AUTHOR _____

CHARACTERS		SETTING

BEGINNING

MIDDLE

END

Kingore, B. (2003). Literature Celebrations, 2nd ed. Austin: Professional Associates Publishing.

STORY MAPPER   _____

Map the story's characters, setting, problem, events, and solution. Use symbols to represent the characters, events, and main idea of the story, and draw a legend.

TITLE _____

AUTHOR _____

TEXT INSPECTOR

Post-it ™ Notes

Inspect the story for passages to read aloud to your group. Use a large Post-it™ Note to mark and number four places to share. Write a few ideas on the note to remember.

TITLE _____

AUTHOR _____

1. In this section, I found:

    ____ a key event.   ____ strong vocabulary.

    ____ a character trait.   ____ figurative language.

    ____ an important setting.   ____ interesting dialogue.

    ____ a surprising twist.   ____ descriptive details.

2. In this section, I found:

    ____ a key event.   ____ strong vocabulary.

    ____ a character trait.   ____ figurative language.

    ____ an important setting.   ____ interesting dialogue.

    ____ a surprising twist.   ____ descriptive details.

3. In this section, I found:

    ____ a key event.   ____ strong vocabulary.

    ____ a character trait.   ____ figurative language.

    ____ an important setting.   ____ interesting dialogue.

    ____ a surprising twist.   ____ descriptive details.

4. In this section, I found:

    ____ a key event.   ____ strong vocabulary.

    ____ a character trait.   ____ figurative language.

    ____ an important setting.   ____ interesting dialogue.

    ____ a surprising twist.   ____ descriptive details.

Tell others in your group which of these is your favorite, and explain why.

Kingore, B. (2003). Literature Celebrations, 2nd ed. Austin: Professional Associates Publishing.

WORD WIZARD _____

TITLE _____

AUTHOR _____

see

ponder

hear

A new word I found is: _____ .

• Its definition in the dictionary is: _____

_____

_____ .

• A synonym of the word is: _____ .

• A antonym of the word is: _____ .

Two interesting words that I want to learn are:

_____ and _____ .

A hard word to spell is: _____ .

Two words in the story that rhyme are:

_____ and _____ .

Four interesting words to use in my writing are:

_____ , _____ ,

_____ , and _____ .

Find examples in the book you read that relate to important skills. (Ask your teacher which skills to list.)

SKILL	EXAMPLES
1. _____	_____ _____
2. _____	_____ _____
3. _____	_____ _____

Kingore, B. (2003). Literature Celebrations, 2nd ed. Austin: Professional Associates Publishing.

READERS THEATER

I made a significant observation my first year of teaching: children love to "ham it up." The one play in the basal reader was the only story the children asked to read again and again. If a play motivated children to want to read, we obviously should produce more plays. Yet the time involved in such productions was too excessive until I discovered readers theater.

Readers theater provides the fun of drama production without the time-intensive pressure of students memorizing parts and preparing costumes or scenery. In readers theater, the emphasis is on communication and the creative interpretation of a story. Since students hold a script and expressively read their parts, preparation for a performance is reduced to students prereading the play and planning together how they will share it with others. Props, signs, or sound effects can be added to the performance, but the goal is to keep it simple. Children usually just stand to read their lines, but simple movements or actions can be incorporated if it helps children have more fun with their production.

Ideas for props:
- Character names on index cards tied to yarn and worn around the neck as signs
- Hats and scarves to wave with a flourish as a character speaks
- Boxes to hide behind and get in
- Chairs or stools to sit on, move around, or represent places
- Cardboard tubes for tree limbs or swords
- Large, simple shapes such as a sun, house, or wolf cut from cardboard and colored with paints or markers
- Masks cut from cardboard or paper plates and colored with paints or markers

---

All children can participate successfully in readers theater. Parts can be expanded to challenge advanced learners or carefully developed to meet the needs of limited English or at-risk learners. Multiple languages can even be cleverly incorporated into scripts.

Begin by helping students work in groups to informally present readers theater plays to one another. Quickly move to sharing performances with other classes. Typically, the performing motivates students to want to do more readers theater. Provide simple scripts such as the ones included in this section. Check the internet for additional scripts and information about using Readers Theater.

Kingore, B. (2003). Literature Celebrations, 2nd ed. Austin: Professional Associates Publishing.

PERFORMING READERS THEATER

Read the script.

Determine each person's part. Several people can cooperatively read one part.

Plan props, if needed.

Consider actions and movements.

Decide if you want to add sound effects or repeat lines.

Practice performing the play together.

Share the play with others.

Have fun!

NOTES

Students Writing Readers Theater

The greatest learning benefits of readers theater result when students interpret literature and write their own readers theater scripts. Then, it becomes an integrated learning experience involving thinking, reading, writing, listening, and speaking. Students in second grade and older can successfully write and perform simple scripts. Short pieces of literature such as picture books, poems, songs, and fables most appropriately fit the process of creating scripts from text. Placing students in groups of two to four insures a rich pool of ideas while encouraging active involvement from all students.

Kingore, B. (2003). <u>Literature Celebrations</u>, 2nd ed. Austin: Professional Associates Publishing.

GUIDELINES FOR WRITING READERS THEATER SCRIPTS

Select the literature.
Brief stories, poems, and even song lyrics can be transformed into readers theater in a reasonable amount of time.

Read and discuss the literature.
Extend your personal understanding and interpretation of the literature to aid its transformation into a script. Discuss what can be left out and what needs to be included most. Analyze characters' feelings and emotions.

Determine characters.
Which characters are essential? Is a narrator needed to explain unspoken parts?

Write lots of dialogue.
The greatest fun is how the character's talk together to tell the story. Have the characters interact and talk the way people you know converse.

Embellish with performance options.
Think about adding simple props, repeating actions or lines, and accompanying certain characters or events with sound effects. What items are readily available that you might use in an unexpected way to add to the fun and effect of your play?

Revise and edit your script.
Consider using peer editing to perfect the final draft of your script.

Rehearse the play.
Read and act out your script several times. Talk together about how to make it more interactive, expressive, and fun.

Perform your play for others.

Kingore, B. (2003). Literature Celebrations, 2nd ed. Austin: Professional Associates Publishing.

NOTES   Begin writing scripts using Aesop's Fables. These short pieces allow students to focus on the process of writing readers theater instead of getting bogged down in extensive text. Several summaries of those fables are included in this section. Challenge students to compare the summary of "The Wind and the Sun" to the completed readers theater script in this section. Analyze and discuss together how the summary was embellished to create a script. Then, students work in small groups to transform another brief fable into a short script. Each group should have a copy of the guidelines for writing scripts to help them organize and sequence the process.

BOOKS

Many picture books provide a good story with dialogue and action possibilities that effectively fit the readers theater format. Stories with humorous elements are particularly attractive to students. The following is a list of student favorites.

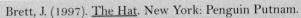

Brett, J. (1997). <u>The Hat</u>. New York: Penguin Putnam.
Celsi, T. (1992). <u>The Fourth Little Pig</u>. Boston: Raintree Steck-Vaughn.
Choldenko, E. (1997). <u>Moonstruck: The True Story of the Cow Who Jumped Over the Moon</u>. New York: Hyperion.
Hoberman, M. (2001). <u>You Read to Me, I'll Read to You</u>. Boston: Little Brown.
Hoffman, M. (1991). <u>Amazing Grace</u>. New York: Dial.
Lionni, L. (1985). <u>Frederick's Fables</u>. New York: Pantheon.
Martin, B. (1983). <u>Brown Bear, Brown Bear, What Do You See?</u> New York: Henry Holt.
Maynard, B. (1997). <u>Incredible Ned</u>. New York: Penguin Putnam.
Scieszka, J. & Smith, L. (1998). <u>Squids Will Be Squids</u>. New York: Viking.
Stephens, J. & Crummel, S. (2001). <u>And the Dish Ran Away with the Spoon</u>. San Diego: Harcourt.
Young, E. (1992). <u>Seven Blind Mice</u>. New York: Philomel.

If students particularly love readers theater, extend the learning experience by integrating some of the related ideas that follow.

1. Audio tape your readers theater productions. Play the tape in the reading and listening learning center, and provide a copy of the scripts.
2. Compile your scripts into a class book.
3. Exchange copies of scripts with other classes to enjoy a wider audience for your children's writing.
4. Perform original readers theater productions for parent night and other meetings.
5. On the internet, contact others who are interested in readers theater. Communicate with them about their ideas for readers theater scripts and productions..

Kingore, B. (2003). <u>Literature Celebrations</u>, 2nd ed. Austin: Professional Associates Publishing.

READER'S THEATER
A-HUNTING WE WILL GO

Interest Level: Grades 1 through 4

1. For each verse, have the children work together to replace the first blank with a type of animal and the second blank with an appropriate rhyming word, eg., goat-boat, fish-dish. Then write out the completed rhyme and perform the readers theater.

2. Each group draws an illustration of the appropriate animal to hold up as they speak.

3. This readers theater can also be performed as a song.

Characters
Group I	Group III
Group II	Group IV

Sound and Action Effects
Stomp feet twice in rhythm following each "A hunting we will go" line.

Group I:	A-hunting we will go (stomp, stomp).
Group II:	A-hunting we will go (stomp, stomp).
Group III:	We'll catch a little
Group IV:	fox
Group I:	and put it in a box
Everyone:	and never let it go.
Group II:	A-hunting we will go (stomp, stomp).
Group III:	A-hunting we will go (stomp, stomp).
Group IV:	We'll catch a little
Group I:	_____
Group II:	and _____
Everyone:	and never let it go.
Group III:	A-hunting we will go (stomp, stomp).
Group IV:	A-hunting we will go (stomp, stomp).

Kingore, B. (2003). <u>Literature Celebrations</u>, 2nd ed. Austin: Professional Associates Publishing.

Group I:	We'll catch a little
Group II:	_____
Group III:	and _____
Everyone:	and never let it go.
Group IV:	A-hunting we will go (stomp, stomp).
Group I:	A-hunting we will go (stomp, stomp).
Group II:	We'll catch a little
Group III:	_____
Group IV:	and _____
Everyone:	and never let it go.
Group I:	A-hunting we will go (stomp, stomp).
Group II:	A-hunting we will go (stomp, stomp).
Group III:	We'll catch a little
Group IV:	_____
Group I:	and _____
Everyone:	and never let it go.
Group II:	A-hunting we will go (stomp, stomp).
Group III:	A-hunting we will go (stomp, stomp).
Group IV:	We've walked more than a mile.
Group I:	Let's sit and watch awhile,
Everyone:	and then, we'll let them go. We want to let them go!

Kingore, B. (2003). <u>Literature Celebrations</u>, 2nd ed. Austin: Professional Associates Publishing.

READER'S THEATER
THE WIND AND THE SUN

Interest Level: Grades 3 through 7

Characters
>Narrator
>Wind
>Sun
>Man

Sound and Action Effects
>Wind - Whooo, whooo
>Sun   - Sizzle, sizzle, sizzle

Narrator: The wind and the sun are having a noisy argument.

Sun: I am certainly the strongest and most powerful of all.

Wind: No, no, Mr. Sun. You are totally silly to even think that you are stronger or more powerful than I am.

Sun: Not at all, Mr. Wind. You are being naive! How could you not realize my strength and power?

Wind: My dear Mr. Sun, everyone who is absolutely anyone knows my strength!

Sun: You certainly can't believe what everybody says. People are very often confused and wrong in what they think.

Wind: You are the one who is confused. How could anyone or anything be stronger than the wind?

Sun: Oh, yes, yes, I agree that you are strong, but the point is that you are not nearly as strong as I am.

Man: Stop arguing you two! I can't get any sleep with all your racket, and I have to work tomorrow!

Wind: It's the stubborn sun's fault!

Sun: It's all the foolish wind's fault!

Man: There you go again with your arguing. This is absurd and getting us nowhere. Tomorrow we will have a contest. I will wear my heavy cloak. Whichever of you makes me take my cloak off is declared the strongest and most powerful.

Kingore, B. (2003). Literature Celebrations, 2nd ed. Austin: Professional Associates Publishing.

Wind: I guess that's fair enough.

Sun: Yes, I guess that's all right.

Man: Good! Now be quiet so I can get some sleep. We'll meet in the field tomorrow at noon. Good night.

Narrator: The man rests; the sun and wind calm down. The next day, they meet at noon.

Man: I see the two of you are ready.

Wind: Oh, yes. I feel so strong!

Sun: Yes, I am ready--ready and powerful!

Man: Good. I am putting on my heavy cloak. Mr. Wind, you go first. See if you can make me take my heavy cloak off.

Wind: Get ready, Man. You won't have that cloak on for long.

Narrator: The wind is so sure of his strength. He huffs and puffs toward the man.

Wind: Whooo, whooo

Narrator: He blows and blows toward the man.

Wind: Whooo, whooo

Narrator: The man pulls his cloak even more tightly around him.

Wind: Oh dear, I'm exhausted! I'm really out of breath! I'm out of wind! How could I have failed to make man remove his cloak?

Man: Looks like it is your turn, Mr. Sun.

Sun: I'm ready, Man.

Narrator: The sun begins to smile, brightens up to his full strength, and shines on the man.

Sun: Sizzle, sizzle, sizzle

Narrator: The sun smiles with an intense beam.

Sun: Sizzle, sizzle, sizzle

Narrator: Soon the man feels so hot he removes his cloak.

Man: You win, Mr. Sun. You are the strongest and most powerful!

All: The moral is: Kindness is more powerful than force.

Kingore, B. (2003). Literature Celebrations, 2nd ed. Austin: Professional Associates Publishing.

AESOP'S FABLES

"The Shepherd Boy and the Wolf"

A mischievous shepherd boy amused himself by calling "Wolf, Wolf!" just to see the villagers run with their clubs and pitchforks to help him. After he called this more than once for a joke and laughed at them each time, they grew angry. One day a wolf really did get among the sheep, but no one believed the boy's cry. The shepherd boy learned that liars are not believed, even when they do tell the truth.

"The Wind and the Sun"

Once upon a time, when everything could talk, the wind and the sun fell into an argument as to which was stronger. Finally, they decided to put the matter to a test; they would see which one could make a certain man, who was walking along the road, throw off his cape. The Wind tried first. He blew, and he blew, and he blew. The harder he blew, the tighter the traveler wrapped the cape around him. The Wind finally gave up and told the Sun to try. The Sun began to smile, and as it grew warmer and warmer, the traveler was comfortable once more. The sun shone brighter and brighter until the man grew so hot the sweat poured down his face. He became weary, and sitting down on a stone to rest, the traveler threw his cape to the ground. You see, gentleness had accomplished what force could not.

"The Goose with the Golden Egg"

Once upon a time, a Man had a goose that laid a golden egg every day. Although he was gradually becoming rich, he grew impatient. He wanted to get all his treasure at once; therefore, he killed the goose. Cutting it open, he found it was just like any other goose on the inside. He learned with sorrow that it takes time to find success.

"The Hare and the Tortoise"

A hare was once boasting about how fast he could run when a tortoise, overhearing him, said, "I'll run you a race." "Done," said the hare and laughed to himself, "but let us get the fox for a judge." The fox consented and the two started. The hare quickly outran the tortoise and, knowing he was far ahead, laid down to take a nap. "I can soon pass the tortoise whenever I awaken." Unfortunately, the hare overslept. When he awoke, though he had ran his best, he found the tortoise was already at the goal. He learned that slow and steady can win the race.

"A Lion and a Mouse"

A mouse one day happened to run across the paws of a lion and awoke him. The lion, angry at being disturbed, grabbed the mouse and was about to swallow him when the mouse cried out, "Please, kind sir, I didn't mean to do it. If you will let me go, I shall always be grateful and, perhaps, I can help you some day." The idea that such a little thing as a mouse could help him so amused the lion that he let the mouse go. A week later the mouse heard a lion roaring loudly. He went closer to see what the trouble was and found the lion he had met caught in a hunter's net. Remembering his promise, the mouse began to gnaw the ropes of the net and kept going until the lion could get free. The lion then acknowledged that little friends might prove to be great friends.

Kingore, B. (2003). <u>Literature Celebrations</u>, 2nd ed. Austin: Professional Associates Publishing.

WEBOGRAPHY

These websites do not necessarily reflect the positions and philosophies of Dr. Kingore or Professional Associates Publishing. They have been research and listed here to serve as a resource. At the time of this book's publication, all websites are accurate and current.

Literacy Websites

Children's Book Council. <www.cbcbooks.org/>

ERIC Reading, English, and Communication. Education Resource Information Center (ERIC). <www.indiana.edu/~eric_rec>

International Reading Association. <www.reading.org>

US Department of Education. www.ed.gov

Internet Libraries

American Library Association. <www.ala.org>

Houston Public Library. <www.hpl.lib.tx.us>

Internet Public Library--Youth Division. <www.ipl.org/youth>

Library of Congress. <www.loc.gov>

LIBSNAP. <http://libsnap.dom.edu>

Los Angeles Public Library. <www.lapl.org>

National Institute for Literacy. <www.nifl.gov>

New York Public Library. <www.nypl.org>

Recommended Reading Lists

Children's choices, teachers' choices, and young adults' choices booklists. International Reading Association. <www.reading.org/choices/>

Reading and books: Recommended reading. New York Public Library. <www2.nypl.org/home/branch/kids/reading/recommended.cfm>

Literature Circles Websites

Literature circles resource center. School of Education. Seattle University. <http://fac-staff.seattleu.edu/kschlnoe/LitCircles>

Recent research on literature circles. <www.literaturecircles.com/research.htm>

Readers Theater Websites

Readers theater for bilingual/ESL students. <http://www.uaa.alaska.edu/uaa/workbooks/readtheater.html>

Readers theater overview. <http://bms.westport.k12.ct.us/mccormick/rt/RTHOME.htm>

Readers theater resources for teachers and students. <http://www.stemnet.nf.ca/CITE/langrt.htm>

Readers theater scripts. <http://falcon.jmu.edu/~ramseyil/readersmine.htm>

Using readers theater with K-2. <http://www.owu.edu/~mggrote/pp/child_lit/c_readers.html>

Kingore, B. (2003). <u>Literature Celebrations</u>, 2nd ed. Austin: Professional Associates Publishing.

REFERENCES

Altwerger, B., Edelsky, C., & Flores, B. (1987). Whole language: What's new? The Reading Teacher. 41, 144–154.

Center for the Improvement of Early Reading Achievement (CIERA). (2001). Put reading first: The research building blocks for teaching children to read. Jessup, MD: National Institute for Literacy at ED Pubs.

Cooper, J. D. (1993). Literacy: Helping children construct meaning. (2nd ed.). Boston, MA: Houghton Mifflin Company.

Daniels, H. (1994). Literature circles. York, ME: Pembroke Limited.

Graves, D. H. (1991). Build a literate classroom. Portsmouth, NH: Heinemann.

Kingore, B. (2002). Rubrics and More! The Assessment Companion. Austin: Professional Associates Publishing.

Kingore, B. (1999). Assessment: Time saving procedures for busy teachers, 2nd ed. Austin: Professional Associates Publishing.

Kingore, B. (1999). Integrating thinking. Austin: Professional Associates Publishing.

Krashen, S. (1993). The power of reading: Insights from the research. Englewood, CO: Libraries Unlimited.

Morrow, L. M. (1989). Using story retelling to develop comprehension. In K. D. Muth (Ed.), Children's comprehension of text: Research into practice. Newark, DE: International Reading Association.

National Reading Panel (NRP). (2000). Teaching children to read: An evidence-based assessment of the scientific research literature on reading and its implications for reading instruction. Jessup, MD: National institute for Literacy at ED Pubs.

Owens, S. (1995). Treasures in the attic: Building the foundation for literature circles. In Hill, B., Johnson, M., & Noe, K., Literature Circles and Responses. Norwood, MA: Christopher-Gordon.

Smith, F. (1990). To think. New York: Teachers College Press.

Strickland, D. S. (1998). What's basic in beginning reading? Educational Leadership, 55(6), 6-10.

Trelease, J. (1995). The read-aloud handbook, 4th ed. New York: Penguin.

Veatch, Jeannette. (1996). From the vantage of retirement: Four areas of reading instruction. The Reading Teacher, 49 (7), 510-516.